Hot-dip G

Hot-dip Galvanizing

*A guide to process selection and
galvanizing practice*

M.J. Hornsby

Published by arrangement with
THE FOOD AND AGRICULTURE ORGANIZATION OF THE UNITED NATIONS
by
INTERMEDIATE TECHNOLOGY PUBLICATIONS
London
1995

Intermediate Technology Publications
103–105 Southampton Row
London WC1B 4HH, UK

© 1995 by FAO and IT Publications

ISBN 1 85339 190 5

Typeset by *My Word!*, Rugby
Printed in the UK by SRP, Exeter

Contents

Figures

Tables

Preface

Steel is by far the most commonly employed metallic engineering material in the world today. It satisfies many of the demands made by the major industries in terms of technical and economic qualities. As always, however, there are limitations on performance; the common engineering steels are not particularly resistant to corrosion. Unprotected steel structures will appear unsightly and covered in rust within days or even hours of exposure to moisture. As steel structures are often load-bearing, prolonged exposure can result in damage to the structural integrity with the consequent cost of repair and replacement.

Galvanizing is just one method of improving the corrosion resistance of steel (and iron alloys) by putting a thin coating on the surface. It has become recognized as a cost-effective solution in a wide range of corrosive environments. It is, however, a manufacturing technology which is relatively capital intensive and requires a healthy respect for its technical, managerial and environmental demands if it is to be used effectively and efficiently. **To set up a galvanizing plant, a sound understanding of science and engineering principles is essential.**

At one time, galvanizing consisted of a steel tank full of molten zinc, kept liquid by an open-hearth coke fire below it, tended 24 hours a day by one man. Steel items would be manually dipped into the liquid zinc, which adhered to the component surface and when cooled to room temperature would provide the necessary corrosion protection. Every four to five months, the steel tank would perforate, sending molten zinc flowing across the floor and employees running to save themselves from burns and worse.

Today, it is not acceptable to subject employees to such dangers, nor is it economically possible to run a business with such losses and inefficiences. The science of galvanizing is now well understood, and consequently the technology continues to be developed to satisfy changing customer requirements in terms of the environment, cost, quality and delivery. Technological improvements almost inevitably increase the capital cost involved, which is of little comfort to a business in an industrially developing country, where access to investment capital is extremely difficult.

It is a simple matter to provide basic data on the basis of which a competent engineer in an industrially developing country could build and operate a small-scale galvanizing plant. There is clear evidence that the innovative activities of such engineers and some organizations have developed and are operating such plants. It is, however, essential to understand the precautions, risks and problems involved. This publication, therefore, attempts to introduce the reader to both the science of galvanizing and the challenges of establishing and managing a manufacturing system safely and effectively.

Objectives of this publication

A common cause of reduced fishing vessel life is reported to be the use of non-galvanized or electro-galvanized fastenings in their construction. This publication discusses the materials and manufacturing aspects of hot-dip galvanizing as part of a production process for improved fasteners.

- Section I gives an introduction to the galvanizing process, its principles and benefits, and the product performance conferred by its use. The latter part of this section is based around the process flow charts used within the galvanizing technology, as this allows general discussion of the choices available to a manufacturing system specifier, such as the types of cleaning and fluxing options and post-dipping processes.
- Section II presents a comprehensive evaluation of a manufacturing unit devoted to the galvanizing of small articles and fasteners with a process specification drawn from the choices discussed, based on an assumed set of requirements. This gives the basis for a business proposal.

This approach is necessary because a manufacturing system specification and its associated costs can only be accurately assessed on the basis of a detailed market evaluation and product specification. In the absence of this data, a series of assumptions must be made. However, the general description of the process options at the end of the first section does allow an engineer to change and adapt the presented specification within the realms of acceptable galvanizing practice to suit his or her needs.

The publication is directed to:

- works managers or foremen interested in setting up and operating small-scale galvanizing plants in industrially developing countries;
- those responsible for the management or use of such enterprises within other businesses, such as boat-yards and foundries.
- field project officers and government officials may also find the information valuable.

Information has been drawn from a range of sources, including international standards and reference publications; a bibliography is appended. The information presented is supported by evidence supplied by practising galvanizers, galvanizing plant suppliers and an affiliate of the international trade organization, the Galvanizers' Association.

It is of limited value to present absolute costs as they remain valid for such a short period of time and are related to specific economic environments. Economic data is presented in a indicative manner, wherever possible relating capital, direct and indirect costs to easily available data.

Acknowledgements

The success of this type of publication relies not only upon the accuracy of the factual information within it, but also on the inclusion of data borne of practical experience. This is of particular importance within the costing exercise when estimates of fluid replacement, maintenance schedules and the like are required. With this in mind I acknowledge the invaluable help offered by the following companies and organizations.

The Galvanizers' Association, Birmingham, UK

Hasco-Thermic Ltd, Birmingham, UK (plant suppliers)

George H. Elt Ltd, Worcester, UK (a small family business with 70 years of galvanizing experience).

Thanks also to the British Standards Institute. Extracts based on BS 729 : 1971 (1986) are reproduced with the permission of BSI. Complete copies can be obtained by post from BSI Customer Services, 389 Chiswick High Road, London W4 4AL, UK; tel. (+44) 181 996 7000.

I am grateful to the Open University for permission to use material from their Manufacturing Management MSc course notes, and to the Galvanizers' Association and Hasco-Thermic Ltd for their permission to reproduce diagrams and data.

Finally, this book would not have been possible without the support and encouragement of Intermediate Technology's Technical Enquiry Service who commissioned the work in response to requests for information to help the fishing industry in industrially developing countries. Information is available on a wide range of subjects from the Technical Enquiry Service, Myson House, Railway Terrace, Rugby CV21 3HT, UK; tel. (+44) 1788 560631.

Introduction

Hot-dip galvanizing is one of a family of metal-coating processes used to protect substrate metal surfaces from corrosion. It is specific to the immersion of steel or cast iron components in a bath of molten zinc after careful cleaning and preparation. Rapid chemical attack of the component surface by the zinc produces a layer of zinc/iron (Zn–Fe) alloys which form a strong chemical bond with the component surface. After removal of an article from the bath, a layer of relatively pure zinc normally remains on the surface and produces a recognizable grey or silvery appearance with an easily identifiable range of patterns, or grain structure, referred to as 'spangle'.

The hard and relatively brittle Zn–Fe layer provides both effective barrier protection and galvanic protection against corrosion. In addition the softer zinc layer protects the component from accidental abrasion and impact during service.

It is generally accepted that for components and fabrications required to operate with minimum or zero maintenance for extended periods of time, often in excess of 20 years, in any of a range of environments, galvanizing is a cost-effective and satisfactory protection system. When shorter operating times are required, or when maintenance is a relatively simple and inexpensive process, the choice of coating system relies on both the operating environment within which the components perform and the economic conditions to which the galvanizing plant is subjected.

Galvanizing is almost exclusively used to describe the production of a zinc coating on steel or cast iron articles by dipping them in molten zinc, and the terms 'hot-dip galvanizing' and 'galvanizing' are therefore used synonymously.

For the purposes of improving continuity in the text, when steel is mentioned, it is used as a generic term describing all commonly galvanized materials including steels and cast irons, unless explicitly stated otherwise.

The process can be applied to a wide range of products, including fabrications, structural steelwork, vehicle parts, nuts and bolts, other fasteners, hollow-ware such as buckets and pans, pylons, bridge girders, roofing sheets, wire and wire products, pipe and conduit, nails, grills, guards and fencing.

Once a typical galvanized coating has been identified, it becomes easily recognizable on many items encountered on a day-to-day basis. Wherever steel is subjected to atmospheric, soil- or water-based corrosion, galvanizing can be considered.

The coating is reliable and can withstand rough treatment. Although it is incapable of reproducing detailed surface finish and therefore imposes limitations on product applications, process modifications can be made to overcome some of these limitations and the technology is relatively simple to deploy in a small-scale industrial environment which benefits from some infrastructural support.

The principles and benefits of hot-dip galvanizing

The term galvanizing has its origin with the concept of galvanic or electrochemical corrosion, which is demonstrated by placing two dissimilar metals in contact with each other in an environment which is electrolytically conductive, such as water or water vapour containing metallic salts in solution.

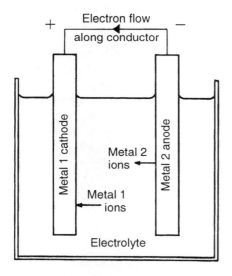

Figure 1: *Galvanic corrosion. Metal ions (charged atoms) of metal 2 are released in the electrolyte. Physically, this results in the loss of metal 2, corrosion. Chemically, as a function of this ionic discharge, electrons are released and flow along the conductor to the cathode, where they are used to combine with metal 1 ions and cause their deposition on the cathode. With suitable metals and electrolytes, electrical loads such as bulbs can be powered by placing them in series with the conductor.*

The principle is the same as that of an electrochemical cell or battery of cells, corrosion being the chemical attack that occurs at the anode. Conversely, batteries make use of the electrical energy produced by such a reaction (Figure 1).

Applying this principle to galvanic protection, metals have individual electrical characteristics known as electrode potentials. The difference between these potentials is the driving force for electrochemical action such as corrosion. When dissimilar metals are connected in the presence of an electrolyte, the driving force for the corrosion reaction is released and electronic conduction (with no mass transfer) occurs by the route of least resistance through the metals from the most electropositive to the most electronegative. To satisfy the requirement for more electrons at the electronegative metal interface with the electrolyte, mass transfer occurs by dissolution of the metal of most electropositive potential, creating ions in the solution.

The main advantages of using zinc are the low melting point (around 420°C) and the fact that zinc is anodic to steel: that is, when in contact with iron or steel in the presence of an electrolyte, zinc will corrode in preference to the iron or steel.

The zinc acts as a 'sacrificial anode' (Figure 2) and corrodes by the mass transfer of zinc ions into the electrolytic solution, releasing electrons to travel the electrically conducting path through the metals to the steel/electrolyte interface where they are consumed in a reverse cathodic reaction, forming compounds with the positively charged ions from the solution. In some instances these deposit as a chemically stable film on the exposed steel or cast iron surface, thereby protecting it from further corrosion and limiting the reaction.

This is of practical importance when areas of steel, normally coated with zinc, are exposed either through mechanical damage of the zinc or through natural corrosive activity of the zinc in a solution and these areas of exposed steel continue to be protected by the surrounding zinc. The value of this process cannot be overstated, as large areas of exposed steel can be protected without subsequent remedial action as long as reasonable areas of zinc remain. Sacrificial protection is the reason why it is possible to internally thread (or tap) steel nuts after galvanizing while maintaining the accurate tolerances required that would otherwise be obliterated by a thick coating of zinc. This exposed steel subsequently remains uncorroded in service.

There is another factor of importance when considering the corrosion activity of zinc. The inherent corrosion resistance of zinc relies mainly on the formation on its surface of insoluble carbonates, which act as a protective film against further corrosive activity. Hence the protection of steel when entirely coated by zinc is a function of the corrosion rate of zinc in a particular environment. There are therefore some

industrial environments where the protective ability is diminished, especially heavily polluted industrial environments in which carbonates are soluble.

For successful coating of steel with zinc by means of galvanizing, a measure of alloying is required at the metal/liquid interface, of which evidence can be obtained by metallographic analysis. A schematic of a typical interface structure is shown in Figure 3. The alloyed interface performs two functions:

- It wets the surface of the steel, allowing uniform coatings to be produced.
- Solidification of the zinc and alloy layers occurs without large differential rates of thermal contraction which could seriously damage the integrity of the coating during cooling.

Although simple in principle, the practice of galvanizing requires careful control mechanisms at each stage of the process to assure a good quality product. Preliminary cleaning of the metal article, fluxing, regulation of bath temperature and the proper use of addition agents, dipping procedure and post-dipping processes all contribute significantly to the quality of the finished product. Maintenance is essential for safe and regular use of galvanizing plant, not least as a major compo-

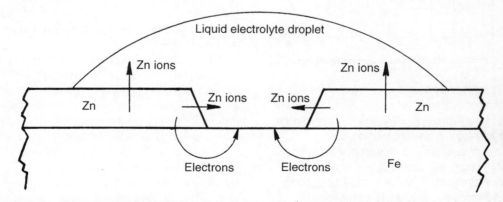

Figure 2: *Galvanic protection. The corrosion reaction at the zinc anode supplies electrons to the exposed steel surface. A cathodic reaction occurs at the steel surface resulting in deposition of atomic species dependent on the compositon of the electrolyte. If the droplet contains acid, then hydrogen would be formed at the cathode surface.*

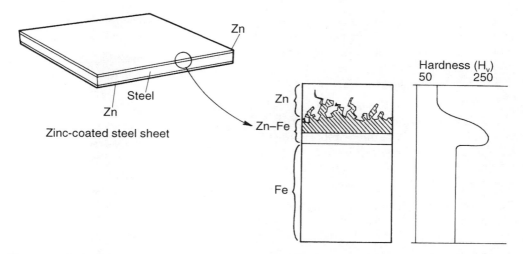

Figure 3: *Schematic representation of a microsection through a galvanized coating. The range of hardness expected for such a coating is also shown.*

nent of the capital expenditure is contained in the body of molten zinc. Perforation of a kettle (as zinc-containing baths are known) is extremely dangerous and costly.

A level of automation is normally used in all but the smallest plants, where the dipping process can be carried out by hand. Only an overhead gantry and a block and tackle are required for rapid transfer of articles through the different stages. The fundamental problems for the galvanizer are cleanliness of the article(s) prior to dipping, and maintaining and controlling a bath of molten zinc for extended periods of time. Careful design of a fail-safe system is also key to successful operation in the finance- and material-constrained environments of industrially developing countries. Rework and scrap can easily become extremely costly to a business.

After adequate cleaning by degreasing and pickling, the steelwork is coated in a flux which removes the oxide contamination of the surface, before immersion in molten zinc held at a temperature within the range of 450 to 460°C or, for high-temperature galvanizing, between 560 and 570°C. This latter process, although used extensively for small fasteners, will not be discussed further as it requires expensive ceramic kettles, and is more technically demanding, generally far more expensive and less efficient.

The steel article is immersed for a period of time between a few seconds and five minutes before being withdrawn, also at a defined rate. During the dipping process 'dross' is produced, a waste product of iron and zinc, which drops to the bottom of the kettle. Dross can lead to waste and potential failure hazard and must be removed at regular intervals.

For small fasteners post-dip centrifuging is essential to remove excess zinc while it is still molten. It is then very common to quench small articles in water (boshing) to impart a shiny, well-spangled finish.

Zinc resists corrosion in most common industrial and engineering environments, from polluted atmospheric conditions to total immersion in sea water. In fact, the sacrificial protection afforded to steel in sea water is maximized because of the excellent nature of sea water as an electrolyte. Arguments for the ecological aspects of the technology are based on the extension of service life imparted to articles by virtue of their coating. This implies that conservation of the natural resources and energy both in high volume manufacture and in maintenance is significant. This must, however, be balanced with the effects of the by-products of the galvanizing process, which include hazardous chemicals and some heavy metal contamination. Conscientious treatment and disposal are paramount.

The technology is generally split into two specific areas:

- *continuous galvanizing* which deals with the automated, high-volume production lines required by the wire-making and automotive industries;
- *general or batch galvanizing*.

This book concerns itself solely with general galvanizing.

Alternative coating systems

There are some variants within the zinc coating family, such as sherardizing (tumbling of components in hot zinc powder), and electro-plating of zinc. These methods, however, offer inferior corrosion properties. Hot-dip galvanizing has two main advantages:

- the coating is much thicker and is alloyed to the surface;
- the alloy thickness builds up at edges and corners as a result of the alloy formation, whereas on conventionally coated components the thickness is significantly less at these regions.

In addition to zinc-based systems, there are several competing technologies which cannot be dismissed:

- metal spraying
- polymer sealing
- organic zinc-rich paints
- inorganic zinc-rich paints
- zinc silicate paints
- drying oil-based paints (primer/undercoat/finish)
- silicone alkyd paints
- two-pack epoxies, primers and undercoats
- one-pack chemical resistant paints
- bitumen and coal tar products.

These alternatives will not be discussed further, but it is pertinent to mention that, in industrially advanced economies, galvanizing is very often selected as the preferred system not only because of the corrosion protection but also because of the high labour requirements of other coating systems, both for initial coating and remedial maintenance. Alternatives may well become more attractive when labour costs are not as high.

The major product variables and their effects on the coating performance

Coating thickness

The ability of a zinc coating to protect a steel component, however applied, is related to the amount of zinc present and its coverage of the exposed steel area. For a dipped article with total coverage, the protective life of the coating is proportional to the thickness of the zinc coating. An important aspect of galvanizing is that the mass of zinc which alloys and coats an article is directly linked to the thickness of that article and its surface area because of the nature of the interfacial reactions. The weight of zinc coating can easily be translated into a thickness because of the uniform nature of the coating produced. The nature of the dipping process, under reasonably constant manufacturing conditions, almost automatically produces a constant coating thickness. Table 1 describes the minimum coating thicknesses to be achieved from base steel component thicknesses when operating to the manufacturing specification of BS729 (a British Standard accepted by industry).

There are three major methods of altering the coating thickness.

Table 1: Coating thickness and steel thickness relationship

Base sheet thickness	Minimum average coating weight g/m^2	Coating thickness μm
≥5mm	610	85
≥2<5mm	460	65
≥1<2mm	335	47
Iron castings	610	85
Centrifuged items	305	43

Surface roughening to increase nominal coating thickness

If the surface of a component is abraded by different means, such as grit or shot blasting, the surface area of the component can be increased by up to 50 per cent. Upon dipping, the increase in surface area leads to a significant increase in coating thickness.

Centrifuging (spinning) to decrease nominal thickness

This process is used on small fasteners and other articles when reasonable tolerances have to be maintained. Immediately after dipping, before the surface layer of unalloyed zinc has had time to solidify, the components are placed in a centrifuge and rotated at 400-750 rpm to remove the liquid zinc and reduce the coating thickness.

Altering the composition of the steel to decrease or increase nominal thickness

The amounts of certain alloying elements, especially silicon, can be varied to alter the coating thickness. The effects can sometimes be unpredictable and complex, and are discussed in the section on materials.

Operating temperature

A galvanized component can comfortably withstand service temperatures of up to 200°C, with short excursions up to 275°C but, above this, degradation is observed by peeling of the zinc-rich outer layers leading to reduced life. Any corrosive activity will be more aggressive with an increase in temperature.

If adequate protection of the component can be achieved with just the Zn–Fe alloy layers, then it is possible to subject it to temperatures up to 530°C but the integrity of the steel is then very much in doubt. The coating will also withstand temperatures down to -30°C.

Mechanical contact

Grit- or shot-blasting of galvanized coatings is possible, for example, to aid painting. However, care must be taken not to be too aggressive as cracking and loss of adhesion/cohesion of the zinc and brittle alloy coating can occur. The avoidance of angular iron grit and pressures of less than 40 psi is recommended.

Otherwise the coating is fairly resistant to mechanical contact, and is tough and abrasion resistant. This is often a significant reason for selecting it. Abrasion studies have reported that a galvanized coating can be 400 times better than an equivalent conventional paint or zinc-rich primer.

Corrosion

As the coating thickness is normally uniform on an article, and because zinc tends to corrode in a uniform manner, lifetimes of galvanized articles can be predicted reasonably accurately for different corrosive environments. Figure 4 shows this relation-

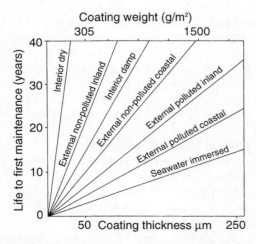

Figure 4: *The life of galvanized coatings.* (Source: British Standards Institute)

ship for a range of common corrosive environments and the thickness of the coating. Other conditions which are worthy of attention are detailed below.

Hot water

In most cases, protective ability is not radically affected by hot water. However, in certain circumstances above 60°C, zinc can become cathodic to steel, and the steel substrate becomes the sacrificial anode, reversing the protective action and accelerating the corrosion of the steel.

Under ground

The contact of zinc coatings with clinker or ashes in the ground should be avoided, as should contact with soils of pH levels below 5.5 and above 12.5. In these cases, a bitumen coating on top of the zinc is recommended.

Wood

Contact with acidic hardwoods should be avoided, but it is interesting that the corro-

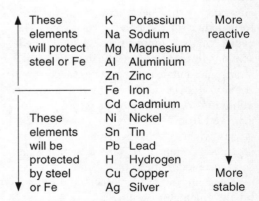

Figure 5: *The Galvanic Series. The order of these elements is based on electrochemical standard measurements. The order may change slightly if the electrolyte composition changes. Other physical attributes of an element may make it unsuitable as a galvanic coating. Aluminium forms an impermeable oxide immediately upon contact with air. The relevant protective coating becomes inert Al_2O_3, and has no value as a sacrifical anode.*

sive action of wood on steel, as happens with nails, is a reason for galvanizing.

Other metals
Bimetallic (electrochemical) corrosion may occur if zinc makes contact with other metals in the presence of an electrolyte, but typically zinc will corrode fairly slowly and uniformly. The larger the gap between zinc and the other metal as shown by the galvanic series (Figure 5), the greater the driving force for corrosion, with the metal closest to the top of the list acting in a sacrificial manner. The order in which these metals are listed, however, depends to a large extent on the electrolytic composition.

Strongly acidic and alkaline conditions
As the slow, uniform nature of the corrosion of zinc relies on the production of impermeable layers of stable compounds on its surface, conditions where these cannot be maintained, such as in strongly acid or alkaline environments, should be avoided.

Paints
Contact with mercury or copper containing anti-fouling paints should be avoided.

Materials

Steel
The versatility and strengths of steel are largely related to their carbon content. This can range from 0.08 to 1 per cent with just about anything in between. Low alloy steels include other metallic elements, almost always in similar or lower proportions. Higher alloy steels contain higher proportions of metallic alloying elements to confer specific physical and mechanical properties, such as chromium (up to 18 per cent) and nickel (up to 8 per cent) to produce stainless steels and cobalt and molybdenum for extremely high strength. The combinations are almost limitless.

Steels used for galvanizing usually contain carbon contents of less than 0.15 per cent and belong to the group of steels normally termed mild or plain carbon steels. However, steels of up to 0.4 per cent carbon have been galvanized without difficulty. Composition is chosen on the basis of economic factors mainly, as mild and plain carbon steels are at the bottom of the price range. In industrially developing countries, identifying metallic compositions can often present problems, because the stock being used for articles has been cast from remelted scrap or has been manufactured from scrap or stock of unknown composition.

Embrittlement of an article after galvanizing can occur if an article has been heavily deformed while cold, such as by cold forging or cold rolling. Typically, the materials from which the article has been manufactured will be over 3mm thick and susceptible to strain ageing because of a high nitrogen content from the original steel-making process.

Cast iron
Cast iron typically has much higher carbon contents, between 2.4 and 4 per cent, which makes it a reasonably simple alloy to produce when compared with steel. Iron casting is still an emerging technology, especially in parts of Africa. Other important alloying elements include silicon (Si), phosphorus (P), sulphur (S), manganese (Mn) and chromium (Cr). It is necessary to maintain low phosphorus and silicon contents to avoid brittleness in the cast iron surface layers after galvanizing; typical contents are 0.1 per cent phosphorus and 1.2 per cent silicon by weight. A common problem with galvanizing cast iron is the surface pick-up on the cast component of silicon from the sand moulds used in sand casting. This surface silicon will promote rapid interfacial reaction between the component and the zinc at these points and will result in brittle and thick Zn–Fe layers. Embrittlement of cast iron can occur if there is a high phosphorus content. To avoid this, components may be heated to 600°C and quenched in water before galvanizing.

The effects of the alloying elements and impurities on the galvanized coatings are interdependent and relate both to the

Table 2: The effect of individual alloying elements

Element	Effect	Action
Carbon		
<0.2%	virtually no effect on coating at normal galvanizing temperatures (450˚C)	
>0.2<0.3%	thicker Zn–Fe layers	
>0.3%	further reaction rate increase	reduce temperature and/or add small amounts of aluminium to the zinc bath to reduce reaction rate
Silicon		
<0.02%	little or no effect	
>0.02<0.09%	increasing Zn–steel reaction rate and thicker alloy layers	
>0.09<0.25%	decreasing rate of reaction leading to thinner coats	0.15 to 0.25% considered normal
>0.25%	reverse trend to thicker coats	reduce temperature and/or add small amounts of aluminium to the zinc bath to reduce reaction rate
Chromium		
up to 0.6%	reported to increase thickness in cast irons	
>4%	reported to decrease thickness	
heat- and corrosion-resistant steels	behaviour similar to that of mild steel	
Nickel		
>5%	reduces or even eliminates the ability to form Zn–Fe layers	maintain below 5%
Hydrogen		
	causes disruption of the coating by outgassing at the interface	good steel-making practice
Manganese		
0.3<1.0%	considered normal	avoid high levels in conjunction with high silicon
Sulphur and Phosphorus		
only important when remelted or contaminated steels are galvanized	increases thickness at areas of segregation	avoid segregation in steels

molten zinc bath temperature and to the time of immersion. Figure 6 shows a common relationship between immersion time and thickness of the coating, assuming a constant bath temperature and different material compositions. Although the amount of zinc on the surface of the low-carbon steel (0.13C) does not increase significantly with dipping times over 4 min-

utes, this is clearly not the case for the medium-carbon steel (0.35C). This illustrates the importance of controlling both the composition of the materials being galvanized and the processing conditions. The rate of attack of the steel by the zinc will determine the ratio of zinc alloy to zinc and therefore the brittleness of the coating (alloy is brittle) and its appearance.

Fabricated articles

Fabrications using different material compositions which are to be galvanized after fabrication may present problems. Specifically, soldered joints cannot be galvanized and brazed joints are difficult to coat successfully. Welding of components of different materials may produce a variation in coating thickness and appearance.

Just as importantly, pickling (acid removal of scale and oxide during the preparation of the component prior to dipping) is a function of composition, and the wrong duration could lead to pitting attack of some parts of a fabrication and/or unsatisfactory de-scaling of others. In this case grit-blasting is preferred as a cleaning method.

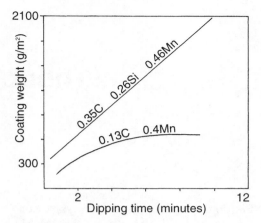

Figure 6: *The relationship between time of immersion and resulting zinc coating thickness for two types of steel (bath temperature 455°C).*
(Source: Galvanizers' Association, UK)

Product design

Finishing processes should always be considered and selected during the product specification and design stage. This avoids unforeseen complications and the need for design changes as there are some product forms that are difficult or impossible to galvanize well. The design of articles also has a significant effect on the plant design. The overall geometry of any workload or component to be dipped must of course be accommodated within the dimensions of the zinc kettle. With items larger than the kettle, double-dipping techniques have been used. For instance, long steel bars can be dipped one end at a time. Just as importantly, however, the facilities of the cleaning and preparation stages must also be capable of accommodating the workload.

The surface areas and the production volumes of articles will determine the rate of use of consumables, the most expensive being the zinc. The required capacity of the zinc kettle is therefore determined both by the geometry of the articles to be dipped and by the throughput. Too high a production volume will not only demand frequent replenishment of the zinc but, more importantly, will cause excessive heat removal, which in turn places greater demands on the heating system. Too low a throughput will result in poor utilization and wasted energy, as a galvanizing plant operates typically 365 days per year with shutdowns only once every two years. Consequently, if the mix and volume of articles for dipping are predictable, a galvanizing system should be designed to optimize its energy efficiency.

General recommendations when designing a product for galvanizing

- Use a good, clean metal with sound construction. A galvanized coating will not adequately cover flaws in workmanship.
- Avoid sharp edges, blind holes and deep recesses wherever possible.
- If galvanizing a fabrication of dissimilar metals requiring different pre-dip treatments, attempts should be made to galvanize before assembly.
- Crevices should be avoided to minimize the seepage of chemicals from rolled, spot-welded, riveted or similar joints. This can lead to corrosion and/or appearance problems.
- Design in smooth clean lines to promote uniform coating behaviour and to avoid accumulations of chemicals or zinc in pockets.
- Avoid galvanizing sealed components, such as sealed box sections, as the expansion of any gases present inside the box during dipping at 450°C may cause an explosion with serious safety implications.
- Provide holes for drainage in inaccessible areas.
- Avoid large section changes or variation in thickness of the article to be dipped.
- On mating surfaces and movable parts, design extra clearance to accommodate the coating thickness; 1mm is adequate.

Specific recommendations

Threaded fasteners

As a general rule, bolts down to M8 (i.e. the nominal diameter of threaded portion is 8mm) can be adequately galvanized. Threaded components up to 4 metres long and 90mm in diameter have also been successfully coated.

Good practice requires that standard sized bolts are galvanized after the thread is formed. To accommodate this zinc coating on the bolts, blank nuts are tapped oversize **after** galvanizing. The internal thread is then lightly oiled to maintain a rust-free surface prior to assembly. The galvanic action of the zinc in contact with the uncoated threads eliminates any corrosion. Figure 7 describes the method of calculating the necessary oversize clearance for the tapping operation. As spinning or centrifuging of the bolts is a standard practice, the thickness is less than that normally obtained, which minimizes the oversize necessary.

ISO, METRIC, UNF, UNC THREADS (Angle = 60°) require increase by

$$2BC = \frac{2t}{Sin\frac{x}{2}} = 4t$$

and for BSW and BSF (angle = 55°) = 4.33t
Increase in effective diameter of an external thread is shown by triangle ABC: AB=t
BC=$\frac{1}{2}$ increase in effective diameter

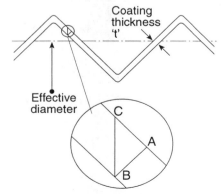

Figure 7: *Calculating allowances for threaded fasteners.*

High-strength friction grip bolts

The same procedure can be followed as for threaded fasteners. However, galling (roughening) of the zinc can occur in the threads because of the high loads involved during assembly, so beeswax or a lubricating grease should be applied.

Welding

Satisfactory welds can be made on galvanized articles, although the welding process is slower and spatter is increased. If welding is carried out before galvanizing, care must be taken to remove any slag, as otherwise bare spots will occur. Gas-shielded welding systems are preferable. If welding is done after galvanizing, adequate remedial protection and repair work must be carried out. Any welding should be continuous on heavy sections but intermittent on sheet of 2mm thickness and over. For thinner sheet, weld at 100mm intervals.

Castings

Pickling baths cannot remove the silicon deposits normally present on the surfaces of sand-cast articles. To avoid the problems associated with high silicon levels during dipping, these deposits must be removed by grit-blasting, or at the very least by thorough manual cleaning with wire brushes.

Distortion

The solidification and cooling of castings produces significant thermally induced stresses. These residual stresses are also introduced into steel components and fabrications during welding or cold forming. Upon subsequent heating and cooling, these stresses are released and can manifest themselves as distortion of the component. The dipping process temperature can also initiate distortion. Effort must therefore be made to minimize the likelihood of distortion by adequate product design or by stress relief prior to dipping. In certain situations, components can be jigged to stop any relative physical movement of the component during the thermal cycle. Furthermore, poor or slow dipping practice can cause distortion by creating large temperature differentials

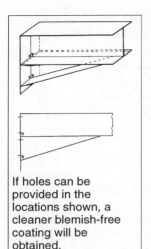

If holes can be provided in the locations shown, a cleaner blemish-free coating will be obtained.

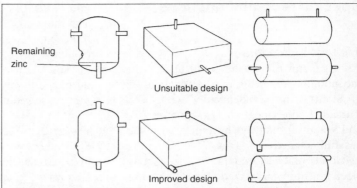

Remaining zinc

Unsuitable design

Improved design

Holes should be positioned at the highest and lowest points on the section to ensure that no air is trapped during immersion and that drainage is completed during withdrawal from the zinc bath. Internal bosses should be omitted wherever possible.

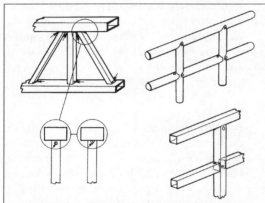

On vertical members, drilled holes or V notches should be diagonally opposite each other and as close as possible to the sealed end.

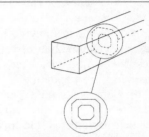

Sections incorporating internal diaphragms and end flanges must also be properly vented. With small rectangular hollow sections, the four corners of the diaphragm plates should be cropped. Larger hollow sections should incorporate an additional 'manhole' at the centre of the diaphragm

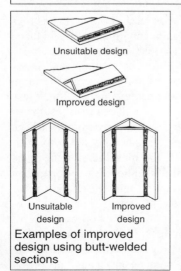

Unsuitable design

Improved design

Unsuitable design   Improved design

Examples of improved design using butt-welded sections

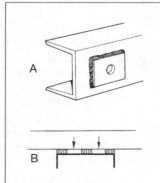

A

B

Venting an area enclosed by the continuous welding of a reinforced plate (A)

If this is not possible, stitch welding should be used (B)

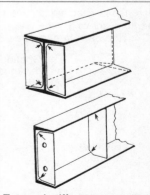

External stiffeners on open sections should incorporate cropped corners or drainage holes to eliminate 'dead pockets'.

Figure 8: *Design recommendations.* (Source: Galvanizers' Association)

in the component, so the designer should consider the need for rapid immersion.

Attempts should be made to design components symmetrically, avoiding large changes in section, and to consider carefully the size and position of drainage and lifting holes and lugs.

Labelling and marking
Permanent marking requires large, heavily punched or embossed marks but, for temporary identification purposes, water-soluble paint or detachable metal labels are adequate. Oil- or enamel-based paints are not suitable.

Masking
Areas to be left uncoated can be masked off with either a specialist high-temperature masking tape or high-temperature greases or paints.

Filling, venting and drainage
Internal areas of hollow items should be easilty penetrated by the molten zinc, and excess zinc and gases should be able to flow out again easily. Without adequate drainage, excessive amounts of zinc can be trapped, resulting in high zinc consumption.

Figure 8 shows some of the more common problems and solutions associated with the design of fabrications.

Connections
Galvanized articles can be joined by welding, adhesive bonding, riveting and bolting.

Handling
The size, shape and volume of articles for galvanizing will determine the method of handling during the process. In some cases holes or lugs will be required to suspend the components on racks or other jigging arrangements. For smaller articles, chains or baskets may be used where no design changes are necessary.

Prior to dipping, the design of an article must lend itself to easy handling without contamination of the surface.

The galvanizing process: stages and options

This section describes the sequence of steps that must be performed to produce a satisfactorily galvanized component. In addition to preparation, there are six fundamental stages of the process: cleaning, pickling, fluxing, drying, dipping and post-dipping.

Within each of the stages there are numerous specific techniques from which to choose. The choice of technique will depend on the product specification, volume requirements and the technical and economic constraints within which the manufacturing process has to operate. As these requirements have not been defined, Figure 10 presents a map of the different options and general standardized descriptions of each activity.

Preparation

This stage is concerned with the division of articles into batches for galvanizing and the methods employed to wire them up or otherwise place them on the handling mechanism of the plant. For mixes of small items this stage is simple, requiring only that the articles are placed in baskets ready for cleaning. For other components it may be necessary to wire or hang them from a suitably designed frame (Figure 9).

Cleaning and degreasing

Typically an alkaline degreasing treatment is necessary to remove oil and grease residues, such as cutting oils from earlier manufacturing processes. If castings, components or fabrications made from scrap are to be galvanized, then silicon deposits,

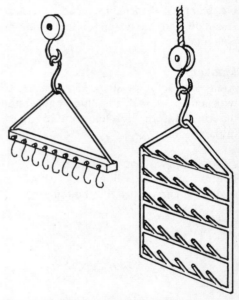

Figure 9: *Typical handling arrangements for components to be galvanized.*

slag from welding and paint must be removed, often necessitating abrasive cleaning. Although Figure 10 suggests either degreasing or grit-blasting, there are some cases where both will be necessary. If the deposits are very easily removed and volumes are low, it may be possible to use manual wire brushing in place of grit-blasting. In some cases degreasing can be avoided, any light oil contamination being removed during dipping by using a thick flux blanket.

There are other cleaning processes, including vapour degreasing, acid cleaning/degreasing and a number of abrasive techniques, but in the majority of cases the

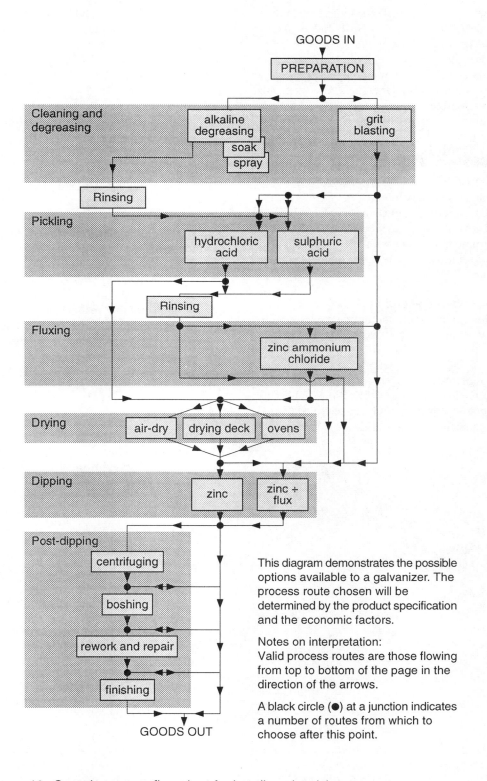

GOODS IN

PREPARATION

Cleaning and degreasing
- alkaline degreasing
  - soak
  - spray
- grit blasting

Rinsing

Pickling
- hydrochloric acid
- sulphuric acid

Rinsing

Fluxing
- zinc ammonium chloride

Drying
- air-dry
- drying deck
- ovens

Dipping
- zinc
- zinc + flux

Post-dipping
- centrifuging
- boshing
- rework and repair
- finishing

GOODS OUT

This diagram demonstrates the possible options available to a galvanizer. The process route chosen will be determined by the product specification and the economic factors.

Notes on interpretation:
Valid process routes are those flowing from top to bottom of the page in the direction of the arrows.

A black circle (●) at a junction indicates a number of routes from which to choose after this point.

Figure 10: *Generic process flow chart for hot-dip galvanizing.*

17

ones described here are entirely adequate and are the simplest to use and maintain. *Solvent degreasing is not recommended* as it redistributes the contaminant as a thin continuous grease film on the product, is environmentally damaging, and demands strict safety equipment and procedures to maintain operator safety.

Alkaline degreasing (including rinsing)

A hot alkaline solution is the most common and effective degreasing process used in general galvanizing where a mix of work is common. It deals with most oily deposits and can be effective in removing some paint.

Plant and equipment

The fundamental requirement is for containers of a suitable size which are resistant to hot alkaline solutions, can be drained safely at regular intervals, and are insulated against heat loss (Figure 11). The most common are steel fabrications, although suitably covered brick, concrete, or wood containers may also suffice.

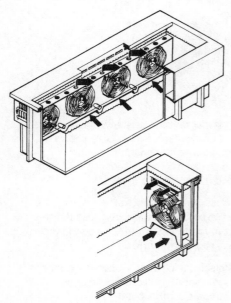

Figure 11: *Typical degreasing plant and heating by steam coil (pumped hot water)*. (Source: Hasco-Thermic)

Rinsing tanks are required for holding both hot and cold water, and again steel fabrications are the most suitable. Holding tanks of similar construction, but coated with acid-resistant glass-reinforced epoxy resin or plastic (GRP) and of larger size, will be required for alkali neutralization prior to disposal. Temperature-measuring and control equipment is necessary.

Power supply

The bath temperature can be maintained by immersing mild steel steam coils into the solution. If oil or gas is used to maintain the zinc kettle temperature, these coils are supplied with water heated by the waste combustion gases from the zinc heating process via a heat exchanger. Temperature control is achieved by controlling steam flow through suitable manual or automatic valve arrangements. If an electrical power supply is used, an appropriate immersion heating element in conjunction with an appropriate 'hi-low' type of controller fitted with thermocouples can replace the steam coil.

Consumables

Alkaline solutions are available in proprietary compositions with full operating and safety data. Suitable solutions can, however, be made from locally available materials. The following compositions are considered satisfactory:

- light oil removal:
  0.5–1.0 per cent detergent in water at 60°C
- heavy greases, paints, lacquers and varnishes:
  5kg NaOH (sodium hydroxide or caustic soda) in 45 litres water.

Sodium carbonate is also used extensively, is less costly and less dangerous than sodium hydroxide, and is used in similar proportions.

Typically wetting agents (soaps) are added to aid cleaning, along with water softeners if the local water contains significant proportions of limestone.

Operating conditions

Hot alkaline degreasing is carried out at temperatures between 65 and 90°C. The duration of immersion of the workload can vary between 1 and 20 minutes, depending on the level of contamination. Typically less than five minutes is required, and agitation can reduce this further. For detergent cleaning, solution temperatures are maintained at 60°C.

After cleaning, it is essential to rinse at least twice (unless detergent has been used where rinsing is not required). The first rinsing bath is maintained at 40–60°C and the second at room temperature. It is not good practice to use the same rinsing equipment as that used to rinse after pickling as these become slightly acid with normal use and scum can form on the surface of the bath.

If adequate rinsing is not achieved, then carry-over of the alkali to the pickling baths will result in rapid deterioration of acidity and hence effectiveness of the pickling process.

Maintenance

Regular preventative maintenance is required to maintain an effective degreasing process and safe operation. As mentioned above, sludge deposited at the bottom of the tank must be removed by pumping at regular intervals. The solution is rarely changed. The regularity of this procedure will very much depend on the volume and cleanliness of the work being processed. Topping-up of the bath should be conducted in accordance with the alkali supplier's data or, if using a made-up solution, the alkali should be added, with adequate agitation, to the water in amounts that do not cause the temperature to exceed 70°C. If this temperature is exceeded a violent exothermic reaction may occur.

The rinsing tanks need not be connected to a water supply, but such a connection would facilitate topping-up when necessary. The baths do not require continuously flowing water but care must be taken to assure the neutrality of the water. During normal usage, scum will form on the surface of the alkali bath, which should be removed by scraping at regular intervals.

Maintenance checks

- Inspect tanks for leaks at regular intervals.
- Thoroughly clean tank interiors every time solution is changed.
- Clean steam coils annually.
- Clean temperature control instruments every time solution is changed.

Health and safety

Hazard Caustic soda is corrosive to all body tissues in all concentrations, and contact can cause dermatitis in low concentrations/low exposure conditions and serious burns in cases of high exposure/high concentrations.

Acute poisoning is normally confined to the area exposed.

Chronic poisoning normally results in dermatitis if exposure to weak solutions is maintained over long periods of time. If swallowed, hospitalization and stomach washing is normally required.

Precautions Employees handling caustic materials and those working in the vicinity of the baths must wear eye, face and body protection, as these solutions can cause severe burns of the body and blindness if in

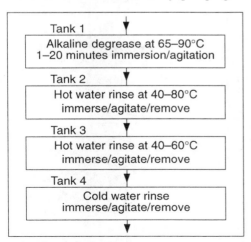

Figure 12: *Process flow chart with operating parameters for alkaline cleaning.*

contact with the eyes. Face shields, safety goggles, rubber or PVC gloves, aprons and boots are considered suitable.

Appropriate procedures for authorization to use caustic materials and adequate training in operation and emergency procedures should be imposed. Arrangements for skin drenching (showers) and eye washing must be made. The degreasing operation must be conducted in a well-ventilated area where fumes cannot collect, so if necessary extraction systems should be installed, as inhalation can cause serious injury.

Environmental issues
Dumping of untreated alkaline solutions will result in contamination of the water table and local rivers. By suitable maintenance scheduling, the used acid from the pickling process can be mixed with the used alkaline solution to effect neutralization of both. According to the rule:

$$Acid + alkali = salt + water$$

solid salts will be precipitated out and will settle on the bottom of the tank; the water can be safely run off. If a suitable disposal route for the salts cannot be found, then careful and secure storage must be made on site.

Abrasive cleaning by grit-blasting
With this process, abrasive iron or steel particles are directed at the components to be galvanized at high velocity, driven either by air or water at high pressure. The impact of the particles on the surface removes surface contamination such as rust, mill-scale, welding slag, and paint.

The need for this type of plant is dependent on the type of product being blasted and the volume. As the equipment is specialized, it will require significant investment, as well as operating and maintenance costs. The major use of grit-blasting is for sand castings prior to galvanizing, where any surface contamination by sand must be removed. If a reliable surface finish can be obtained, the components can sometimes be transferred directly to the galvanizing bath with a flux blanket, thereby removing

the need for pickling. To be able to omit pickling entirely from the process, however, is very unlikely.

Plant and equipment
A range of plant is available, from large open chambers within which appropriately protected employees blast the components using a hosepipe arrangement, to small bench-top units managed by an operator remaining outside an enclosed space but, with hands protected by rubber gloves inside, handling the component and controlling the direction of the abrasive flow (Figure 13). The process can be quite slow.

For small-scale and low volume work, grit-blasting guns, similar to paint-spraying guns with specially hardened surfaces, can be used, connected to a portable air compressor.

Power supply
The pressures involved demand electrically driven air or water compressors.

Consumables
The grit is normally recycled, but regular supplements will be required to replace loss. The effect of the abrasion makes nec-

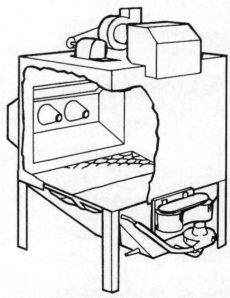

Figure 13: *A cabinet-type abrasive cleaner.*

essary the regular replacement of shields (especially transparent ones), protective clothing, and pressure nozzles.

Operating conditions

Operating conditions will be entirely determined by the type of component and the level of contamination. Pressures used are normally in excess of 60 psi.

Maintenance

The maintenance required will be determined by the level of use, but primarily involves visual inspection, topping-up with grit, changing of worn parts and routine lubrication of pump parts if necessary.

Health and safety

Hazard The pressure of the air can cause embolism (air bubbles introduced into the bloodstream which inevitably cause death if they reach the heart). The other obvious hazard is damage to the body by exposure to the high-velocity grit.

Precautions Avoid all contact of the pressure nozzle on the skin and wear protective clothing. Rubber is normally acceptable.

Alternative methods of paint removal

In specific instances, where degreasing or grit-blasting processes are not suitable for removal of paints, either proprietary paint-stripping solutions can be manually applied followed by rinsing, or components can be dipped into the zinc kettle followed by stripping of adherent zinc by immersion in the acid bath, and then normal pickling. This is termed 'burning-off'. Obviously, this must be avoided on a regular basis as contamination of the acid and zinc wastage occurs.

For less severe cases, manual wire brushing may be acceptable. However, maintaining a consistent quality of work is very difficult.

Pickling

Pickling is the method by which mill-scale and rust is removed from the surface of the components and requires the use of acid solutions. In galvanizing, hydrochloric acid

(HCl) and sulphuric acid (H_2SO_4) solutions are almost exclusively used. Sometimes, if castings are being processed, hydrofluoric acid (HF) solutions may be employed, but this is particularly hazardous and expert advice should be sought. The aim of the process is to remove the surface scale without attacking the underlying steel surface (overpickling). This demands the use of inhibitors in the solutions which reduce the amount of zinc pick-up and give a better surface finish. Furthermore, the rate at which the iron (Fe) content builds up in the pickle (which impairs its ability to descale) is reduced. In modern plants, pickling is normally the first process to be conducted on the premises, the degreasing having been completed by the component supplier. The acid selected for the pickling medium will be based on the plant design, the availability and condition of acid and the capability of local industry to recycle or dispose of the solutions. The advantages and disadvantages of the two solutions can be summarized as shown in Table 3.

Plant and equipment

Pickling containers of a suitable size are required which are resistant to acid solutions and which can be drained safely at regular intervals. With HCl pickling, two, three or even four separate tanks may be required, containing different concentrations of acid. The most common are steel fabrications coated in acid-resistant GRP, although rubber-covered brick, concrete, or wood containers coated with wax and assembled with fasteners made from suitably corrosion-resistant materials may also suffice.

Unless the 'old dry' process of fluxing is employed exclusively (see page 26), cold water rinsing tanks will be required. Again

---

Important safety procedures

- Always add acid to water.
- Do not add acid to hot solutions.
- Avoid splashing.
- Impose thorough rinsing procedures.
- Neutralize spent solutions prior to disposal.

Table 3: Process characteristics

Process characteristics	HCl	H_2SO_4
cost of acid (arbitrary units)	1	0.5
fumes	ventilation or fume suppression	extraction required
operating temperature	room temperature	60–65°C
overpickling	unlikely	greater possibility
tolerance to Fe build-up	high	lower
rinsing	simple or none required ('old dry' flux process)	requires thorough rinse
operator safety	safe	less safe
heating costs	none	significant
material composition	better for steels>0.6%C	better for steels <0.6%C
speed of pickling	slower	faster
number of tanks required	higher	lower
acid regeneration	difficult and expensive	cheap and easy
present usage	most common	less common

GRP-coated steel is a cheap and effective solution. Unless running water is used, iron salts will quickly build up in the rinse tank. Preferably two rinse tanks should be used, with water running from the first tank (which is continually fed with fresh water) into the second. Holding tanks of similar construction but larger size will be required for acid neutralization prior to disposal. However, these tanks will also suffice for the alkali neutralization required by the degreasing process and a standard design will allow interchangeability at a later date if necessary.

For sulphuric acid pickling, only one tank is normally required, made from the same materials but with the presence of lead steam coils to maintain the temperature of 60–65°C. In some plants sulphuric acid pickling will precede hydrochloric acid pickling.

Power supply

No power supply is required unless bath heating is specified, in which case the same method as for alkali degreasing can be employed using lead-clad heating coils.

Consumables

Both H_2SO_4 and HCl solutions are available in prepared proprietary compositions with full operating and safety data. Suitable HCl solutions can however be made from commercial grade (27.5 per cent by weight) acid solution plus inhibitors such as bran flour, glue, petroleum sludge, gelatin, animal wastes or coal and wood tars in the proportion of 0.25 per cent of the weight of acid. In addition to inhibiting the corrosive attack on the steel, they also reduce fume and acid consumption. The following apparatus is required to monitor the HCl composition:

- small glass funnel
- 25ml graduated cylinder
- 250ml graduated cylinder
- 50ml burette
- 250ml conical flask
- methyl orange indicator
- sodium carbonate solution
- hydrometer covering the range 1.0–1.3 specific gravity (S.G.) or 0–60 Tw
- filter papers

HCl can often be supplied by oil refineries at low cost as a by-product from their operations. Regenerated HCl (green in colour) is also a cost-effective source available from chemical suppliers. Adequate supplies of water must be maintained.

H_2SO_4 is supplied either in the form of BOV (brown oil of vitriol) consisting of 75–78 per cent H_2SO_4 or COV (concentrated oil of vitriol) consisting of 95–97 per cent H_2SO_4. The pickling solution is normally made up to 10–14 per cent of acid in water.

Operating conditions

HCl pickling

The concentration of hydrochloric acid is not critical, but the temperature is. Below 15°C HCl pickling is very slow. If a temperature of 18–21°C is achieved, the nature of the exothermic reaction of the scale with the acid will maintain that temperature. If overnight cooling is a problem, heating by steam injection may be necessary. The duration of immersion of the workload can vary between one and 20 minutes, although if no inhibitor is used this can be reduced to

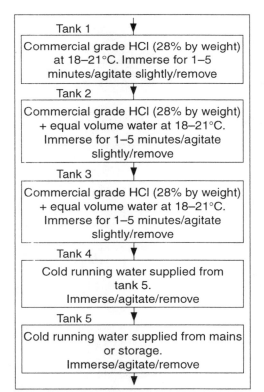

Figure 14: *Typical process flow chart with operating parameters for HCl pickling.*

less than a minute for some steels, depending on the level of scale and rust. Slight agitation should be employed although this increases fume generation.

After pickling, it is essential to rinse thoroughly unless the 'old dry' process of fluxing is used, where the components are hung above the pickle bath to dry or are placed directly on a drying deck. During normal usage, the iron content of the bath will rise and normal evaporative and carry-out losses will occur.

Maintenance of pickling baths

Regular preventative maintenance is required to maintain effective pickling and safe operation. Topping-up of the solution can be carried out in accordance with the acid supplier's documentation, or by adding solutions of the same concentration. When making up these solutions, care must be taken to **add acid to water** rather than water to acid, to prevent explosion. The nature of the pickling process is to dissolve iron salts, and ultimately these will accumulate to such a degree in the solution as to render it ineffective. This point is reached when the iron content reaches 80–100g per litre. Additions to the solution should be stopped when the measured iron content reaches 50g/litre. Rather than dispose of the acid, it can be used as a stripping solution for rework or cleaning of components already partially covered with zinc. The control of the acid is carried out routinely, and the equipment used to measure the composition can also be used to monitor the effluent when discharged to the sewerage outlet.

Monitoring of iron content

Use the hydrometer to measure the density of the pickle liquor and pick off the iron content from the nomogram shown in Figure 15 after determining the acid content.

Health and safety

Hazard Undiluted commercial grade HCl will produce severe burns on skin and eyes. Inhalation is unlikely to be a serious problem because the irritant nature of the gas

23

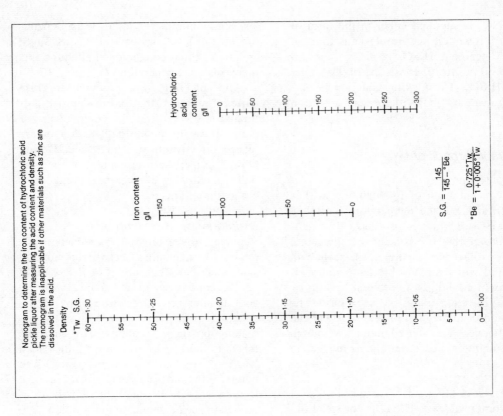

Nomogram to determine the iron content of hydrochloric acid pickle liquor after measuring the acid content and density. The nomogram is inapplicable if other materials such as zinc are dissolved in the acid.

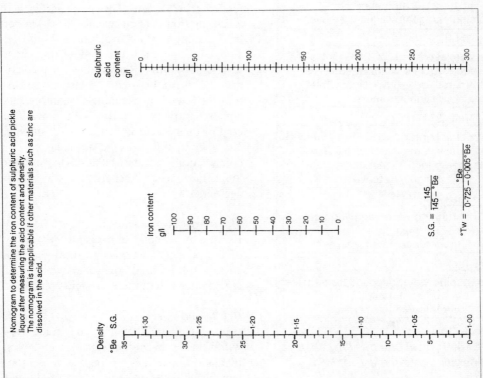

Nomogram to determine the iron content of sulphuric acid pickle liquor after measuring the acid content and density. The nomogram is inapplicable if other materials such as zinc are dissolved in the acid.

Figure 15: *Nomograms to determine iron contents of H_2SO_4 and HCl.*

24

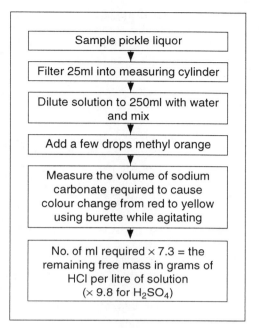

```
┌─────────────────────────────────┐
│   Sample pickle liquor          │
└─────────────────────────────────┘
              ▼
┌─────────────────────────────────┐
│ Filter 25ml into measuring cylinder │
└─────────────────────────────────┘
              ▼
┌─────────────────────────────────┐
│ Dilute solution to 250ml with water │
│            and mix              │
└─────────────────────────────────┘
              ▼
┌─────────────────────────────────┐
│  Add a few drops methyl orange  │
└─────────────────────────────────┘
              ▼
┌─────────────────────────────────┐
│   Measure the volume of sodium   │
│   carbonate required to cause    │
│  colour change from red to yellow │
│   using burette while agitating  │
└─────────────────────────────────┘
              ▼
┌─────────────────────────────────┐
│   No. of ml required × 7.3 = the │
│  remaining free mass in grams of │
│     HCl per litre of solution    │
│        (× 9.8 for H₂SO₄)         │
└─────────────────────────────────┘
```

Figure 16: *Monitoring of free acid content.*

makes continued work in dangerous concentrations intolerable.

Acute poisoning Inhalation causes severe respiratory problems. Contact with eyes and skin causes immediate burns and pain.

Chronic poisoning Inhalation of low concentrations causes erosion of teeth, bleeding and ulceration of gums and nose, and redness and tenderness of skin.

Precautions Employees handling HCl, and those working in the vicinity of the pickling baths, must wear eye, face and body protection. Face shields, safety goggles, rubber gloves, aprons and boots are considered suitable. Adequate natural ventilation should be provided and the process enclosed if possible.

Appropriate procedures for authorization to use HCl and adequate training in operation and emergency procedures should be imposed. Arrangements for skin drenching (showers) and eye washing must be made.

H_2SO_4 pickling

Pickling with sulphuric acid is essentially the same as HCl pickling, except that tem-perature must be controlled. The acid and iron contents are measured in the same way as for HCl, but for free acid content replace the 7.3 in the calculation (shown in Figure 16) with 9.8 to determine the mass/litre of H_2SO_4. Recovery units can be installed within galvanizing plants to recycle the spent H_2SO_4.

Maintenance checks

- Inspect tanks for contiguity of the protective coating at regular intervals.
- Thoroughly clean tank interiors every time solution is changed.
- Clean steam coils annually.

Health and safety

Hazard H_2SO_4 in various concentrations will produce severe burns on skin and eyes. Acid mist and fume is strongly irritant to eyes, nose and mouth. Permanent eye damage is possible, and is likely by direct contact with liquid. Permanent blackening of teeth is possible.

Precautions Employees handling the acid, and those working in the vicinity of the pickling baths, must wear protective eye, face and body protection. Face shields, safety goggles, rubber or PVC gloves, aprons and boots are considered suitable. Adequate ventilation should be provided and the process enclosed if possible. High temperature operation requires mechanical fume extraction and scrubbing as the fumes will be highly corrosive. Appropriate procedures for authorization to use, and adequate training in operation and emergency procedures should be imposed. Arrangements for skin drenching (showers) and eye washing must be made.

Environmental issues

Dumping of untreated acid solutions will result in contamination of the water table and local rivers. By suitable maintenance scheduling, the used alkali from the degreasing process can be mixed with the used pickle liquor to effect neutralization of both. The resultant salts precipitated out will settle on the bottom of the tank and the water can be safely run off. If a suitable disposal route for the salts cannot be found, then careful and secure storage must be made on site.

Fluxing

To produce a satisfactory uniform zinc coating requires that the zinc and steel surfaces react. Even after the degreasing and pickling treatments, oxides and other impurities will remain or form. The action of the flux is to remove these last barriers to reaction and to maintain that cleanliness until the article is dipped in the zinc. Figures 17, 18 and 20 describe the three processes of fluxing used by galvanizers.

There is ongoing debate over the most satisfactory method of fluxing; however, it is fair to say that the 'old dry' process is considered to give unreliable and inconsistent results. Selecting either the 'dry' or the 'wet' process will depend mainly on the geometry and the mix of work the galvanizing plant will process.

The 'old dry' process

The pickle salts act as the flux and are produced by allowing the article to dry after the HCl pickle. Typically, a basket or hanger of work will be left hanging above the pickle tank to dry before being taken to the dipping tank. This process cannot be used with any other pickle solution (see Figure 17).

Plant and equipment

None required. The only specific requirement is that the pickling process uses HCl and there is a capability to dry the work. If drying above the pickle bath is not satisfactory then either a drying deck or an oven will be required; refer to the plant and equipment section relating to the dry process. It is very unlikely that a business considering the purchase of an oven would rely on this process for fluxing, given the level of investment required. Indeed, it is likely only to be of use as a standby process if another fluxing system is non-operational but work has to continue.

Power supply

None required.

Consumables

Refer to the section on HCl pickling.

Operating conditions

Refer to the section on HCl pickling. After pickling, the components must be thor-

Table 4: A comparison between the 'wet' and the 'dry' fluxing processes

Process characteristic	'Wet' process	'Dry' process	Comments
zinc consumption	higher	lower	if aluminium present in zinc bath
dross formation	higher	lower	if aluminium present in zinc bath
flux residue on article	some	less	causes poor appearance
process equipment	none	fluxing baths, drying ovens and control equipment	drying oven expensive
component geometry	no restrictions on size, volume or shape	uniform if oven used	
non-value-added zinc loss	7%	27%	the 'dry' figure can be reduced to 11% if recycling carried out
production rate	high	lower	unless both systems used and drying omitted
sensitivity to preparation	lower	higher	flux blanket has stronger cleansing action

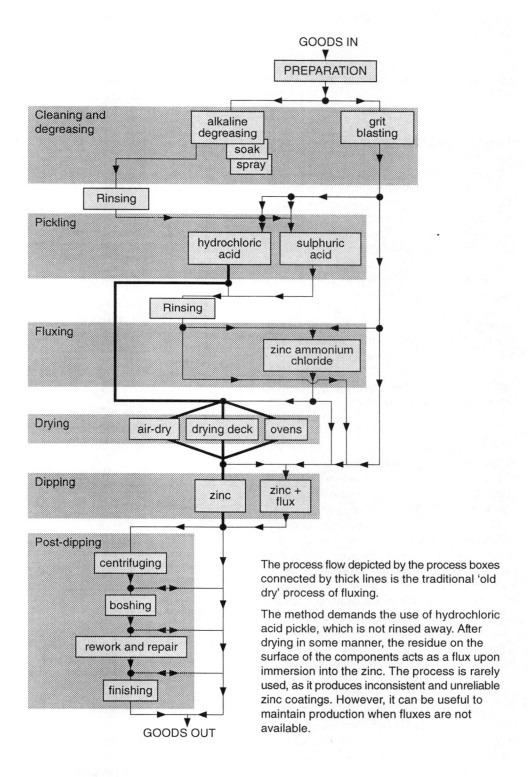

GOODS IN

PREPARATION

Cleaning and degreasing

alkaline degreasing

soak

spray

grit blasting

Rinsing

Pickling

hydrochloric acid

sulphuric acid

Rinsing

Fluxing

zinc ammonium chloride

Drying

air-dry | drying deck | ovens

Dipping

zinc

zinc + flux

Post-dipping

centrifuging

boshing

rework and repair

finishing

GOODS OUT

The process flow depicted by the process boxes connected by thick lines is the traditional 'old dry' process of fluxing.

The method demands the use of hydrochloric acid pickle, which is not rinsed away. After drying in some manner, the residue on the surface of the components acts as a flux upon immersion into the zinc. The process is rarely used, as it produces inconsistent and unreliable zinc coatings. However, it can be useful to maintain production when fluxes are not available.

Figure 17: *The 'old dry' process of fluxing.*

oughly dry before immersion in the molten zinc, to avoid dangerous splashing and poor coverage of the work by the zinc.

For maintenance, health and safety, and environmental issues, refer to the section on Pickling.

The dry process

After thorough rinsing to remove the iron salts and the residual acid, the components to be dipped are 'prefluxed' by immersing them in a bath of aqueous zinc ammonium chloride. The components must then be transferred either to a drying deck or ovens where they are dried thoroughly before immediate dipping in the molten zinc. It is important to note that a significant part of the fluxing (or cleaning) process occurs during drying, and therefore care must be taken to ensure that it is carried out efficiently. The amount of flux deposited on the surface of the components is a function of the flux concentration, and the cleaning performance is a function mainly of the drying time and temperature (see Figure 18).

Plant and equipment

A container of a suitable size is required which is resistant to acid solutions, can be drained safely at regular intervals and is safe to use at temperatures up to 80°C. The most common are steel fabrications coated in glass-reinforced epoxy resin or plastic (GRP), although rubber-covered brick, concrete, or wood containers coated with wax and assembled with fasteners made from suitably corrosion-resistant materials may also suffice. Prefluxing above room temperature aids the drying process. To facilitate regeneration of used flux, an auxiliary container will be required of the same or larger dimensions and a pumping system, either by syphon or mechanical methods.

Drying decks are heated perforated cast iron or steel plates. The components are typically shovelled on to these plates before returning them, dried, into baskets for dipping. Otherwise, gas- oil- or electrically fuelled ovens are required of specific size and shape to accommodate the racked or basketed components.

Power supply

Preflux If the preflux solution is to be used above room temperature then heating arrangements such as described for hot alkaline degreasing (page 18) are suitable. Drying decks are normally heated by the waste gases from the zinc kettle (not electrically heated) passing the underside of the plate.

Consumables

Preflux solution Proprietary mixes are available which are mixed with water as required. There are two other methods for obtaining a satisfactory solution:

- zinc ammonium chloride ($ZnCl_2,3NH_4Cl$) + 1 per cent of a suitable wetting agent such as glycerine, tallow or a carbohydrate + equal weight of water.
- zinc chloride salt ($ZnCl_2$) + ammonium chloride (NH_4Cl, 'sal ammoniac') + wetting agent + ammonium hydroxide (NH_4OH) + water in order to produce a solution of specific gravity (S.G.) 1.15–1.16.

For example, 1020kg NH_4Cl + 969kg $ZnCl_2$ salt + 8 litres wetting agent in 6000 litres of water. An adequate water supply must be maintained.

The solution is expensive and tends not to be changed very often. In fact carry-over and other losses are generally replaced with fresh solution. If the solution is changed it is not treated but removed for specialist treatment and disposal.

Operating conditions

The components are immersed in the flux solution, held at a temperature within the range of 18 to 80°C, immediately removed and dried, either in an oven held at a temperature within the range of 120 to 200°C for approximately two minutes or on a drying deck held at a similar temperature.

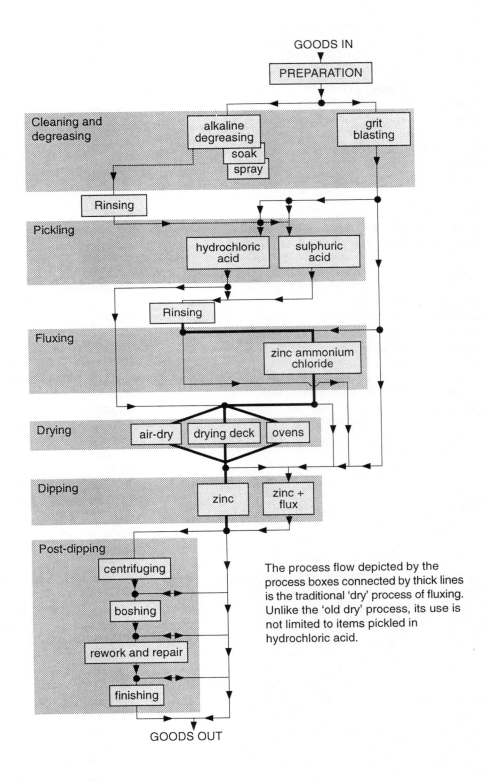

The process flow depicted by the process boxes connected by thick lines is the traditional 'dry' process of fluxing. Unlike the 'old dry' process, its use is not limited to items pickled in hydrochloric acid.

Figure 18: *The 'dry' process of fluxing.*

Dry galvanizing must be used if aluminium is present in the molten zinc in excess of 0.007 per cent unless cryolite is available as a flux addition (10 per cent by weight). The aluminium is added to confer flexibility to the zinc coating of the article and to reduce oxidation of the hot zinc surface in contact with the atmosphere. If wet fluxing is used the aluminum will be scavenged from the bath by the flux, resulting in waste of both flux and aluminium.

Maintenance

Again, maintenance checks for the integrity of the flux baths are made by visual inspection. The maintenance of the preflux solution requires tests for free acid content, specific gravity and visual inspection of the solution for the identification of sludge formation, which indicates a high iron salt content. Iron can be removed by pumping or syphoning the solution into an auxiliary tank and then treating it with hydrogen peroxide. After standing for several hours, the clear solution can be pumped back into the original tank. Topping-up of the solution

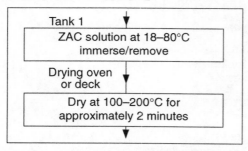

Figure 19: *The process flow chart for dry galvanizing.*

should be with water and chemical additions should be made to maintain the specific gravity of the original solution. Generally speaking, 200g flux per litre of water provides a solution of approximately S.G. 1.10. The free acid content is measured in the same way as the pickle solution, but the titration of the sodium carbonate is made directly into a 100ml sample of the flux solution. The titration result (in ml) multiplied by 0.1825 then becomes the free acid content in grams per litre HCl. When this

level exceeds 2g/litre in the solution, the flux solution should be neutralized by adding ammonia solution or zinc ash.

Maintenance checks

- Tanks should be inspected for contiguity of the protective coating at regular intervals.
- Tank interiors must be thoroughly cleaned every time the solution is changed.
- Steam coils should be cleaned annually.

Health and safety

The zinc ammonium chloride should be treated in the same manner as any acid. The guidelines for HCl pickling are therefore applicable.

The wet process (flux blanket)

This process does not require any process plant, as the flux floats on the surface of the molten zinc. Cleaned and pickled work can therefore be passed through the blanket (as it is called) of flux, and immediately immersed in the zinc without the need for drying. Upon removal, the flux wipes excessive zinc off the component, allowing a faster withdrawal rate and consequently a faster production rate. However, if this method is used, quenching (boshing) of the components must be carried out to remove all traces of the flux residue. This process is favoured for workloads that consist of small fasteners and mixes of sizes and shapes, and when spinning (centrifuging) is to be carried out. In some cases, galvanizing plants will employ both a flux blanket and a preflux bath to speed up production by avoiding the need for drying.

During operation, flux skimmings need to be removed from the surface of the bath, or possibly from between the surface of the bath and the blanket. Although skimmings contain up to 50 per cent zinc, in the form of shot-like particles, it can only be resold at a low price. They also contain various chloride salts. The high iron content of the

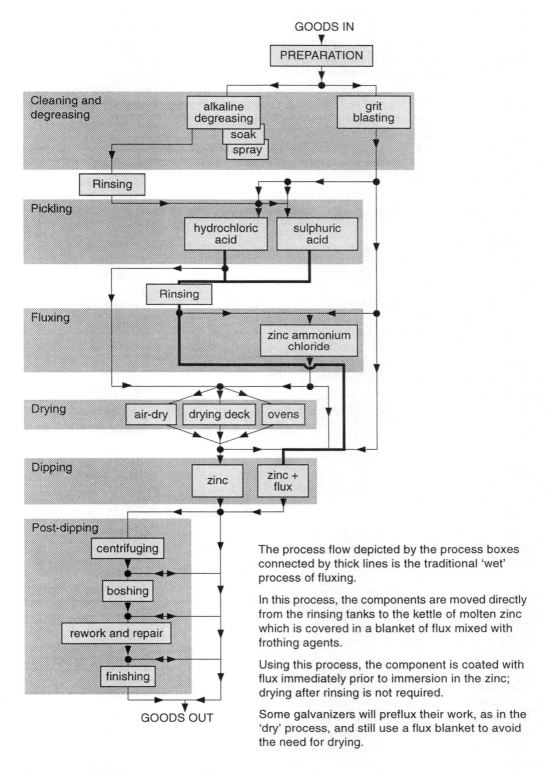

GOODS IN

PREPARATION

Cleaning and degreasing

alkaline degreasing
soak
spray

grit blasting

Rinsing

Pickling

hydrochloric acid

sulphuric acid

Rinsing

Fluxing

zinc ammonium chloride

Drying

air-dry | drying deck | ovens

Dipping

zinc

zinc + flux

Post-dipping

centrifuging

boshing

rework and repair

finishing

GOODS OUT

The process flow depicted by the process boxes connected by thick lines is the traditional 'wet' process of fluxing.

In this process, the components are moved directly from the rinsing tanks to the kettle of molten zinc which is covered in a blanket of flux mixed with frothing agents.

Using this process, the component is coated with flux immediately prior to immersion in the zinc; drying after rinsing is not required.

Some galvanizers will preflux their work, as in the 'dry' process, and still use a flux blanket to avoid the need for drying.

Figure 20: *The 'wet' process of fluxing.*

31

zinc (2 per cent), however, means that the metallic zinc cannot be returned to the bath after separation without specialist reclamation processes. Depending on the economics of the galvanizing plant being installed, it may be cost-effective to incorporate such a reclamation plant to produce metallic zinc (low iron), zinc ammonium chloride and zinc oxide. The zinc oxide can be resold and is used in creams and paints.

Plant and equipment
Only the galvanizing kettle and ancillary equipment required for dipping.

Power supply
None required.

Consumables
Powdered zinc ammonium chloride (ZAC) and frothing agents such as bran, sawdust or glycerine in percentages of 1 to 2 per cent are required. In the absence of ZAC, ammonium chloride can be used, but it will remove zinc from the bath and creates more fumes upon initial reaction. Mixtures of 65 per cent zinc chloride and 35 per cent potassium chloride have also been used successfully.

Operating conditions
The main conditions of operation are covered in the Dipping section.

The flux mixture is sprinkled on to the surface of the molten zinc where immersion of the articles will occur, and is prevented from covering the whole bath by a weir or paddle arrangement. It is also permissible to cover the whole bath, significantly reducing oxidation of the zinc, improving heat conservation and effective in wiping excess zinc from the components upon withdrawal.

Maintenance
The satisfactory performance of the flux blanket requires that a fluid, thick and continuous blanket is maintained at all times. Initially, sufficient flux should be added to ensure that, if it is skimmed, enough flux remains to re-cover the surface. Over a period of time, the fluidity of the flux will reduce, although for a limited time fluidity can be regained by adding small amounts of ammonium chloride. At the end of each shift, or every eight hours, the blanket should be removed by skimming and placed in empty, clean oil drums. When cold the product is harmless.

Health and safety
Please refer to the section on Dipping.

Zinc chloride and ammonium chloride are caustic substances and protective clothes (as worn elsewhere in a galvanizing plant) must be worn to avoid splashes or other contact with skin and eyes. The fume produced by the contact of ZAC or ammonium chloride with molten zinc is dense but relatively harmless. However, it should be kept to a minimum by using adequate ventilation – either mechanical extraction or a tall chimney stack.

Environmental issues
Unless the skimmings are reprocessed, the ash sold and the zinc and ZAC recycled, the product will have to be suitably disposed of. It is strongly recommended that a properly ratified authority be contacted which can properly and safely dispose of the contents, normally in a landfill site. Zinc is a heavy metal and can contaminate the water table and rivers if incorrectly disposed of.

Dipping
Adequate degreasing, pickling and fluxing allows the molten zinc to react chemically with the steel surface of an immersed component, producing Zn–Fe layers of varying composition and thickness at the interface. If the reaction has been adequately controlled, a layer of zinc with the same composition as the molten zinc will remain on the outermost surface.

The quality of the coating for a particular composition of steel relies on:

- the quality of the zinc
- the temperature of the galvanizing bath

- time of immersion
- rate of withdrawal.

The rate at which the coating thickness increases for temperatures between 445°C and 480°C tends to be parabolic with time, although if high-silicon steels are coated, the rate becomes linear because of continued alloy growth. The withdrawal rate should be slow (1.5 metres per minute is generally accepted) as a faster rate can cause runs and lumpiness of the coating, and unnecessary waste of zinc. However, this speed of withdrawal can be increased substantially if centrifuging is specified, as the excess zinc will be removed and returned to the bath. Slower rates may allow the remaining unalloyed zinc on the surface to react with the steel substrate and form more of the brittle Zn–Fe compounds. A change in rate of withdrawal from 1.5 to 15m/minute can increase a coating thickness by 50–70mm.

Conversely, the immersion rate should be as fast as possible without causing splashing, to expose the whole component to the zinc at the same time and impart a uniform thickness. Generally speaking, the time of immersion can vary between one and five minutes, but a good indication of the time to withdraw is when 'boiling off' has ceased. With normal galvanizing steels, linear growth of the coating stops after about one to two minutes. With silicon steels, immersion time should be as short as possible.

Above 480°C, the coating thickness growth rate will be linear with time on ordinary steels; however, dross formation will be very high and attack of the kettle will be dramatic and will reduce its lifetime to months. Below 445°C the reaction rate becomes very sluggish and inefficient. The optimum temperature is the lowest that allows free drainage of the zinc during withdrawal: between 445 and 465°C.

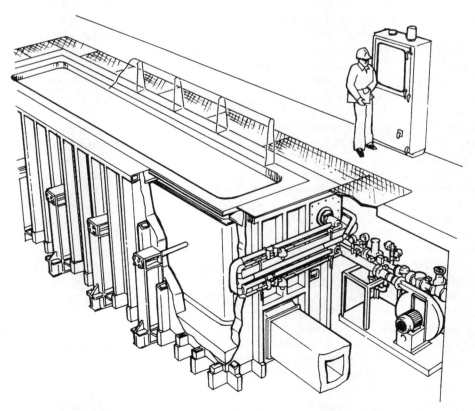

Figure 21: *A large capacity, general galvanizing furnace.* (Source: Hasco-Thermic)

Plant and equipment

Galvanizing tanks, or kettles as they are known, are by far the most important and costly item on the list of plant required (see, for example, Figure 21). It is the only part of the plant that is generally bought in from specialist manufacturers, as the consequences of it failing in service because of inadequate construction, choice of materials or design of heating system are disastrous. Aluminium killed boilerplate steel of 50mm thickness is almost globally used as the kettle material and consists of maximums of 0.08 per cent carbon, 0.02 per cent silicon, 0.45 per cent manganese, 0.025 per cent phosphorus, and 0.03 per cent sulphur, the remainder being iron.

For sizes greater than 2.5 metres long by 2 metres deep, vertical strengthening bars should be used. The welded tank is surrounded by a refractory construction and any of a number of heating systems, oil, gas or electricity, can be employed. The lifespan of galvanizing kettles is reduced significantly by the number of times solidification of the zinc occurs, with shutdown and inspection normally only occurring every two years of continuous operation. When specifying the size of tank, a general rule is to require 20 times the volume of zinc parts to be galvanized in one hour. In practice, this ratio is often found to be nearer 40:1. The tank geometry should be designed to expose the minimum of molten zinc to the atmosphere while allowing free movement of the components or batches of components in and out.

Furthermore, too small a volume of zinc for a given throughput will place greater demands on the heating system as the rate of heat removal becomes too high. It is generally accepted practice to have either enough containers (such as clean oil drums) or a stand-by bath ready to hold the zinc in the event of a failure or other emergency. A zinc pump capable of transferring one to two tonnes per minute is also necessary. The heating system should be designed to minimize convection currents which disturb the dross settling at the bottom of the kettle, and to maintain a constant temperature, both of which facilitate the production of a smooth, uniform coating.

Power supply

Generally speaking, diesel fuel or gas-oil is preferred with forced air blowers and automatic fuel regulation. Temperature control can be monitored and controlled by simple microprocessor circuitry, controlling air flow via a damper valve to the burner unit and using sheathed thermocouples (two minimum) to feed back kettle temperature information. The paramount consideration when choosing energy sources is continuity of supply as kettles typically run for two years continuously before shutdown for maintenance.

Electricity is simplest but may suffer from interrupted supplies, especially in industrially developing countries, requiring high-output cut-in generators and increasing costs. If electricity is chosen, a simple array of resistance heater coils can be attached to the external surface of one side of the kettle wall to provide the necessary heat input. The control system is essentially the same as for the diesel system, but without the need for mechanical control.

Consumables

Zinc

Most commercially available grades of zinc can be used for galvanizing. Often termed gob (good ordinary brand) or prime western, suitable alloys contain a maximum of 1.68 per cent lead and iron. Care must be taken when accepting remelted zinc, as the iron content may be excessively high, resulting in poor performance of the coating process and, more importantly, the large amounts of dross formed are likely to promote kettle perforation by causing hot spots at the base of the container.

Likewise there is no benefit in using high purity zinc as this will accelerate zinc attack of the kettle walls and reduce their working life.

Lead

Traditionally lead has been added to the zinc bath to aid the collection of dross. This was common practice when the zinc baths were heated from the bottom to aid heat transfer. However, this addition is now unnecessary as heating from the sides of the bath walls is accepted practice, avoiding convection currents which disturb the dross.

Aluminium

Aluminium is frequently used as an additive to the baths: up to 0.007 per cent by weight. Up to about 0.005 per cent, it acts to reduce the oxidation losses of the molten zinc at the bath surface, and improve the appearance of the coated article. The addition of aluminium above this amount reduces the reaction rate at the surface of the article, thus reducing the coating thickness, and above 0.007 per cent the dipping process starts to become more difficult to manage. Above 0.03 per cent black spots will begin to occur on dipped articles, representative of uncoated areas. The presence of aluminium above 0.007 per cent when using a flux blanket requires an addition of 10 per cent cryolite to the flux to avoid transfer of the aluminium from the bath to the flux, where it serves no useful purpose. Aluminium is present only in remelted zinc, so once again care must be taken to use a reputable and consistent supplier.

Temperature measuring and control equipment should be considered consumables, and adequate spare components should be available. Most importantly, spare thermocouple elements and refractory sheaths for them should be kept for immediate replacement in the event of failure.

Operating conditions

To facilitate the dipping process, a two-speed hoist attached to an overhead gantry is recommended for all but the smallest manually operated plants. The two speeds of operation allow fast immersion and slow withdrawal and the gantry allows for the work to keep moving through the bath from one end to the other. As the dross produced during operation is denser than the zinc, it settles on the bottom of the kettle, and care must be taken to avoid contact of the workload with it by immersing too deeply.

Disturbance of the dross will cause it to adhere to the surface of the work, producing unsightly surface discontinuities on the final product.

If batches of articles are immersed at the same time, then they should be withdrawn at the same time and not individually, as this would result in a variation of coating thickness, and unnecessary wastage of zinc.

If the workload is being withdrawn without a flux blanket, or ash is evident on the surface of the zinc, the bath must be skimmed prior to removal. If this is not done, the ash will adhere to the surface of the work, causing both unsightly appearance and reduced corrosion resistance. If a flux blanket is being employed, significant reduction in ash formation can be expected, and savings in the amount of zinc consumed because of the wiping effect as the work is removed. After withdrawal through the blanket, the items are moved either directly to a bosh (water quench unit) to remove flux residue, or to a centrifuge. If no flux blanket has been used the workload is cooled as quickly and as uniformly as possible.

Maintenance

Regular attention must be paid to the process control equipment, including:

- checks on thermocouple performance,
- correct temperature measurement by calibration, and
- the regular two-year shutdown and inspection.

In addition, the safe and efficient continuous operation of the dipping process depends largely on the effective management of residuals that are produced during use. The three residuals are dross, ash and flux skimmings.

Dross

A pasty solid consisting of approximately 96 per cent zinc and 4 per cent iron is produced by carry-over of iron-bearing pickle salts, the flux, the articles being galvanized, and iron and steel handling components all reacting with the molten zinc. It is not

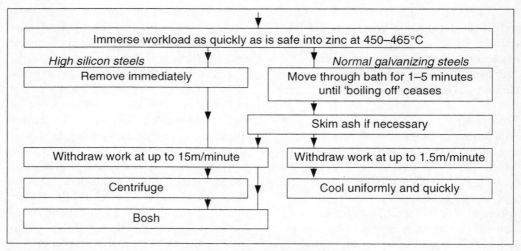

Figure 22: *Typical process flow chart for the dipping process.*

uncommon for articles to be lost in the zinc bath, which also results in the production of dross.

Increasing the temperature of the zinc significantly increases the amount of dross formed in wet galvanizing between the blanket and the zinc, as do too-frequent additions of ammonium chloride and slow immersion times. If no blanket is employed (dry galvanizing), the major cause of dross is the reaction between the workload and the zinc. A 100 per cent increase in the amount of dross formed can be expected by increasing the bath temperature from 450 to 470°C.

The reaction of zinc with the kettle walls is of little significance as layers of protective Zn–Fe alloys are quickly formed and the steel contributes no further part in dross formation unless the temperature exceeds 480°C. Above this temperature, attack is very rapid, which not only produces vast amounts of dross but also reduces the kettle life dramatically. The dross settles to the bottom of the kettle, where, if disturbed, it becomes attached to the workload. Furthermore, as a poor conductor of heat, it can cause hot spots on the kettle wall in areas not available for inspection (Figure 23).

Dross can be removed at regular intervals, normally every 100 or so hours, using either a perforated ladle or a specially designed grabber (Figure 24). If dross is

not removed regularly, perforation of the kettle wall will occur near the base, resulting in the loss of almost all of the zinc and destruction of the kettle.

Dross formation can be minimized by:

• avoidance of overpickling
• low galvanizing temperatures
• maintenance of constant bath temperature
• for wet galvanizing, maintenance of low iron content in the pickle solution
• regeneration of flux blanket only when necessary
• for dry galvanizing, thorough rinsing procedures.

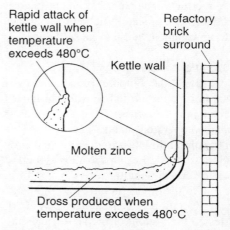

Figure 23: *The effect of dross build-up on kettle floors.*

36

Ash

A mixture of zinc oxide and entrained zinc (zinc is often in excess of 80 per cent of the total weight), ash is produced by the disturbance of the surface of the zinc in contact with air, which entraps zinc in the oxidized zinc film. Incorrect removal of ash can also lead to significant amounts of lost zinc.

Ash formation is not a problem when a flux blanket is used to cover the whole zinc surface, but if the blanket is absent from the withdrawal area, skimming using a wooden blade is necessary to clean the surface. The ash can then be removed using a perforated ladle.

Ash can be treated to reclaim the metallic zinc by partially immersing the open end of a steel cylinder in a corner of the bath and skimming the ash into it. Regular stirring of the contents allows the zinc to drain back and the remaining oxide can be ladled out (Figure 25). If the bath is too small for this operation, a clay–graphite crucible containing molten zinc at about 450°C can be used. With the addition of small amounts of ash and repeated removal of the residue, the zinc content will rise until it can be baled out and returned to the kettle, and the process repeated. About 150kg/hour can be treated this way. A yield of 50 per cent zinc can be expected if the ash is treated immediately.

Flux skimmings

The by-product of the wet galvanizing process, flux skimmings need to be removed when the blanket becomes sluggish. If the flux is removed carefully using a perforated ladle, most of the entrained zinc is allowed to drain back into the bath. However, if a high proportion of zinc remains in the skimmings, one of the processes described for the ash reclamation

may be used. It is common practice to remove and replace a flux blanket every eight hours or at the end of a shift.

Kettle maintenance checks

These are made during the shutdown, normally scheduled every two years. At this time, the zinc is either pumped out or ladled into a holding tank, clean oil drums or ingot moulds and left to cool. The 2–3mm thick Zn–Fe layers on the kettle walls are removed by chipping hammers and discarded. Any dross is removed from the base. Grid lines are drawn at approximately 0.15m intervals on the walls and base, and angle grinders are used to grind back to the steel surface at the grid intersections. When sparks are seen, the steel surface has been reached. It is normal practice at this point to employ ultrasonic thickness measurement equipment to test the integrity of the wall. Careful attention is paid to the swill line (the original surface level of the zinc in the bath), especially if a flux blanket is used. Any repairs are made by welding using electrodes of similar composition.

An empirical formula (see below) is used to determine the wear (reduction in thickness) of the kettle wall in terms of thickness lost.

After inspection and repair have been effected, the kettle should experience a slow rate of increase to temperature while containing slabs of zinc to minimize thermal stresses. Typically this takes four to seven days and is controlled by maintaining a maximum of 50°C difference between the inside and outside of the kettle wall. If oil- or gas-fuelled heating systems are used, regular cleaning and component replacement will be necessary to maintain efficiency.

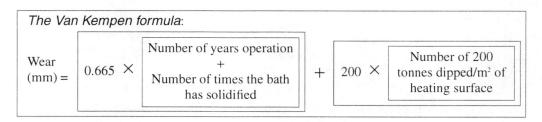

The Van Kempen formula:

$$\text{Wear (mm)} = 0.665 \times \left(\frac{\text{Number of years operation}}{\text{Number of times the bath has solidified}} \right) + 200 \times \left(\frac{\text{Number of 200 tonnes dipped/m}^2 \text{ of heating surface}}{} \right)$$

Health and safety

The major concern is to avoid contact with molten zinc, by:

- wearing adequate clothing including face shields, leather aprons, gloves and shoes
- having adequate run-out ports at the base of the zinc kettle with catch-pits of an adequate size to contain the molten zinc in the event of kettle perforation.

The main source of contact with molten zinc is during immersion of the workload, and care must be taken. Either a dipping screen made from toughened glass should be placed between the operator and the bath or, better still, a full screen enclosure should surround the bath. In its solid state, zinc is innocuous and there are no serious hazards related to its handling. Its boiling point is approximately 900°C, so there is no problem of zinc fume being generated during galvanizing.

Environmental issues

A heavy metal, zinc must not be allowed to contaminate rivers or the water table as it will cause significant damage to flora. Care must be taken to minimize particulate emission of zinc during galvanizing as it will settle on the roofs of adjoining buildings and subsequently be washed off by rain into the rivers.

The disposal of the residuals must be carried out with consideration and all sensible attempts made to recycle. The fumes produced during contact of ZAC with the molten zinc should be collected using mechanical extraction and a bag filter. This will also serve the purpose of collecting zinc and zinc oxide dust.

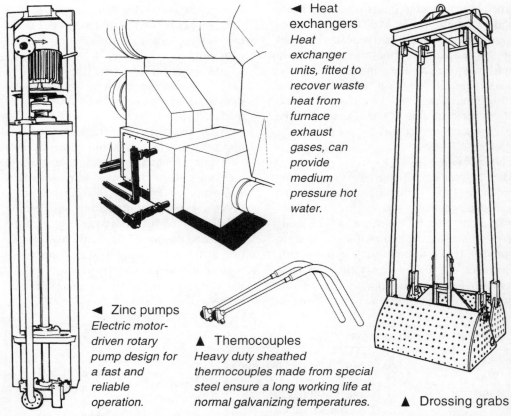

◄ Heat exchangers
Heat exchanger units, fitted to recover waste heat from furnace exhaust gases, can provide medium pressure hot water.

◄ Zinc pumps
Electric motor-driven rotary pump design for a fast and reliable operation.

▲ Thermocouples
Heavy duty sheathed thermocouples made from special steel ensure a long working life at normal galvanizing temperatures.

▲ Drossing grabs

Figure 24: *Ancillary equipment required for galvanizing.* (Source: Hasco-Thermic)

Figure 25: *Reclamation method for ash.*

Post-dipping processes

Centrifuging

Essential for small articles and fasteners handled in baskets where excess zinc would obscure a threadform or other surface feature, centrifuging requires rapid transit of the workload from the zinc bath to a high-powered centrifuge which reaches 300–750 rpm in two to three seconds (Figure 26). The excess zinc is removed within a few seconds and after removal of the workload can be collected and returned to the bath. Immediately after the centrifuge has stopped spinning, the workload is quenched in water in a 'bosh' or quench tank to acquire an aesthetically pleasing shiny appearance.

Quenching or boshing

Boshing can also be carried out on large items with a high heat capacity, to remove any tendency for further alloy growth dur-

ing cooling, and also to remove any flux residues which may contribute to corrosion.

Rework and repair

Components failing inspection or being returned after some time in service will require stripping of the existing zinc before further dipping. This is carried out by using discarded pickle solution and the process is similar to that described in the section on pickling.

If articles require fabrication after galvanizing, specifically by welding, zinc will have to be removed adjacent to the areas to be welded. Also, if damaged or uncoated areas require repair, they will also have to be cleaned manually using a wire brush or by some form of abrasive cleaning. Subsequent recoating can be effected by using zinc-rich paints or low-melting-point zinc alloy solders available in stick, paste or powder form. It is accepted practice to deposit at least the same weight of zinc as was removed since the damage took place.

When welding, apart from the hazards associated with that process, the operator must be protected from the zinc fume produced, as this can cause 'zinc fume fever' in the short term, producing symptoms similar to those of malaria. No long-term effects are known.

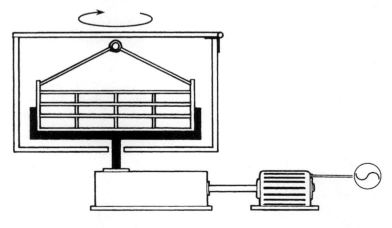

Figure 26: *Certifuge for removal of excess zinc from small articles.*

39

Product quality

Quality can be described as the supply of a product that meets the customer's requirements. This is somewhat different from meeting specifications or tolerances which may not have been designed with that customer's application in mind. This is especially applicable in industrially developing countries where operating conditions for products may be different from those where the standards and specifications were generated.

A specification can generally be considered as a comprehensive document describing the minimum standard of workmanship, the materials and manufacturing methods which will result in a product of consistent quality. British Standard 729 (BS729) has been used as the benchmark in this publication. There are other equivalent or near-equivalent European standards which are broadly similar in their content and are referenced in the bibliography. In order to meet these standards it is especially important to be able to control the various stages of the galvanizing process.

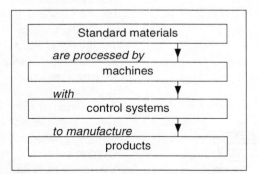

Figure 27: *The four key elements of a manufacturing process.*

The quality of the final galvanized product will be dependent on the level of control exerted over the manufacturing process, which can be broken down into four elements (see Figure 27).

The total quality will depend on the performance of each of these functions. The cost of quality is the sum of the cost of preventing failure, cost of inspecting to identify failure and the cost of failures so identified plus returns from the field. In industrialized countries this total cost commonly ranges from 10 to 25 per cent of a company's annual turnover.

The minimization of quality costs is achieved by concentrating on prevention and therefore eliminating the need for inspection and replacement of failures. In practice this is often not feasible, but by creating a content and motivated workforce, and exercising firm control over the manufacturing system by standardized procedures, regular maintenance and training, a manufacturer can reduce inspection requirements and failures to a minimum. Achieving consistent, high quality output is a substantial foundation upon which further improvements and process innovations can be made. In the context of the four elements described, the product quality is dependent on two factors: external and internal.

External factors

Materials supply
In a competitive marketplace, a manufacturer can move between suppliers, or in the case of sub-contract galvanizing, can refuse

work if the material condition or composition is unsuitable. Clearly this is not the case in many developing countries where the quality of the material being brought into the galvanizing shop cannot be analysed for suitability.

If the galvanizer is working on a jobbing basis, little control is possible, apart from working closely with the customer. The most important issue is to identify failed coatings that are the result of unsuitable material and attempt to trace the material source to a supplier or to a particular product.

If the galvanizing plant is part of a dedicated manufacturing plant, then in addition to working closely with the other manufacturing managers and designers to specify the correct material, attempts should be made to build a good working relationship with the raw material supplier. In both situations there is a need for some form of material selection and validation process.

Product requirements
The supplier must be certain that the requirements set by the customer are attainable, otherwise future business can be significantly affected.

Internal factors

Machines
The galvanizer has much more control as long as consumables and spare parts are available. Machines should be well maintained and operated by a well trained and experienced workforce. Even if this means higher capital investment to include comprehensive training in the early days of operation, it is essential for safe and profitable long-term operations.

Control systems
In addition to the temperature control, acid regulation and other hardware controls, adequate controls must be in place to monitor and direct operations through documented procedures and standards for operation of plant and equipment. This includes work tracking and scheduling of work, and generally what can be called an appropriate management system.

Table 5: Defect descriptions

Defect description	Cause	Action to remedy
dull rough patches	excessive alloy growth	• cool faster after dipping • reduce immersion time • reduce zinc temperature • reduce pickling time
uneven coating	dipping temperature too low/withdrawal too fast	• increase temperature • slower withdrawal
pimples	solid particles adhering to surface during dipping or sand on castings	• remove dross or ash more frequently • modify dipping technique • clean castings more effectively
bare patches	inadequate cleaning or pickling	• ensure cleaning process removes all surface contaminants
blisters	result of laminations on steel surface releasing gas on dipping	• improve design
staining and discoloration	residual flux/pickle residue in laminations	• quench to remove flux • thorough rinse to remove pickle
white rust	storage of newly galvanized products under damp conditions.	• store dry • apply phosphate or chromate conversion coating

Inspection techniques

Assuming appropriate systems are in place and the galvanizing process is under control, a number of inspection techniques are available to identify defects and to assure quality.

The fundamental requirement is for a uniform and continuous coating. Quantitative techniques are available for measuring these parameters including both destructive and non-destructive tests.

- The strip and weigh test is a destructive test used to measure coating weight.
- The Preece test is also destructive and comprises a chemical evaluation to determine coating uniformity.
- Metallographic sectioning, grinding and polishing can be used to determine coating make-up and thickness.
- Non-destructive magnetic induction methods are also available to measure coating thickness.

In the absence of advanced technology quality assurance procedures, simple tests may be developed that provide adequate assurance of coating quality and quantity. When designing and evaluating such tests it is important to be able to compare standardized test results.

The adhesion of a coating can be assessed by a series of light blows with a peening hammer. Other tests are visual and assess the quality of the coating.

Section II – the manufacturing unit

Facility set-up and operational details

This section deals with the specification and costing of a hot-dip galvanizing plant, based on a set of assumptions which are derived from a comprehensive evaluation of the market requirements. Unless the volume, mix, source and general geometries of the parts requiring galvanizing (the 'goods-in specification') and the product specification (the minimum standard to which the work is to be galvanized) are known, the process specification cannot be determined. The data can be simultaneously fed into a suitable economic analysis. If the economics are favourable and funding is available, plant set-up and operations can commence.

There are problems in presenting such an approach in a publication of this nature, as costs change with time and with, most significantly, prevailing economic conditions in different countries. The approach taken for this section, therefore, is to assume a set of requirements and a set of cost figures. The model, built up as described in diagrammatic form in Figure 28, can then be used with data collected from the field.

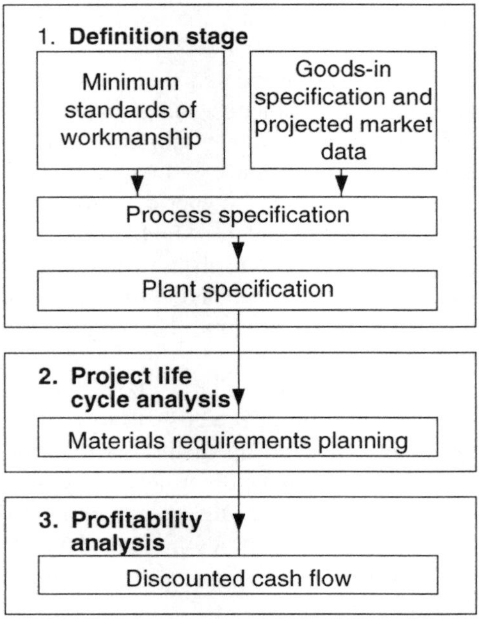

Definition stage

At this point the minimum standard of workmanship (the product specification, such as BS729) is selected, along with a specification of the type of work requiring galvanizing. In addition some market research should have provided projected levels of use for the plant for the lifetime of the project. Once these have been defined, a process flow chart for the galvanizing plant can be determined from the information supplied in Section I. Once these specifications have been obtained, flux methods, kettle size, and so on, can be selected, and the plant specification and layout can be designed.

Project life cycle analysis

The satisfactory operation of the galvanizing plant will require periodic inputs of materials and effort, such as initial investment (the plant specification), maintenance and consumables. These can be planned for the life cycle of the project.

Figure 28: *The model used to determine the feasibility of a hot-dip galvanizing plant.*

Profitability analysis

The profitability of a galvanizing plant is the net cash expenditure subtracted from the net cash revenue, taking into account the initial cost of the investment, the cash expenditure arising and the time value of money throughout the operating life of the facility. This stage is the conversion of the materials requirements identified in stage 2 (see Figure 28) into cash terms.

You need only to apply the cash values relevant to your own particular economic circumstances in the final profitability analysis stage to determine, at a first approximation, the viability of employing this particular process.

It is important to realize that the figures applied in the project life cycle analysis, such as for the rate of consumption of water, or the spares and repairs required over the lifespan of the project, are *estimates*. If there is cause to question the validity of an estimate, then a number of these analyses can be conducted with different values each time. Comparison of the results will demonstrate the sensitivity of the economics to these values. The graphical analysis (Pareto Analysis) describing the proportion of the total costs allocated to each part of the process is also a guide to the critical costs and therefore identifies those items requiring closer scrutiny. The cash figures presented in the example are only representative and do not relate to real circumstances.

The model demonstrates a reasonable method for calculating the economic viability of the system, for a general first-off approximation. Two distinct sets of data are required:
- Capital investment and process specific consumable costs, available from galvanizing plant suppliers, suppliers of zinc, flux etc. For these the plant specification in this publication can be used or one can be created using the information in Section I. There are a limited number of suppliers in the world and, for industrially developing countries, this information may have to be sought overseas.
- Environment-specific costs such as labour rates, utility supplies such as electricity, fuel and water and the charges of local fabrication companies. These costs are available within the environment into which the process is to be placed and therefore they reflect the economic situation of the local area.

The model evaluates only the direct costs of a galvanizing plant, but it is a simple matter to include other relevant overheads that are applicable to particular circumstances in the materials requirements planning stage. Taxation policy is not taken into consideration as this is typically a complex affair and country specific. The appropriate factors may be applied to the individual revenue and costs in accordance with local tax laws.

Once the process specification has been defined, an adequate management system must be put in place to create an effective functional system, dealing with both the engineering and administrative sides of the business, as otherwise the quality of the work and consequently the performance of the business will suffer.

It cannot be overstated that for successful galvanizing practice and a stable business, based on customer satisfaction, to be maintained, the technology know-how must be transferred to the owner/operators. The only parts of the plant which need to be supplied by experienced galvanizing plant suppliers are the kettle and associated heating and control systems. The engineering skills may well be available locally to fabricate the kettle and ancillaries; however, as a major proportion of the cost of a galvanizing plant is locked up in the molten zinc, early failure of the kettle or heating systems as a result of employing an inexperienced engineering firm to produce such plant can easily cause the end of the galvanizing business.

It is generally accepted that, with any manufacturing enterprise, the experience gained by the employees through operation of the plant should result in increased productivity and product quality. Thus the costs of manufacturing reduce with time (notwithstanding inflationary pressures imposed by the economy). This is reflected in the costs of rework and scrap reducing with time. In fact, the 'learning curve' is used in industrially developed countries to demand lower prices of suppliers as time passes. It is relevant, therefore, to recognize that in the early days of plant operation, high rates of scrap and poor productivity are likely and, without adequate support services, this is unlikely to improve significantly, so the operation will not achieve its full potential.

Definition stage

Goods-in specification and projected market data

The products for galvanizing will be small forged or machined fasteners, mainly nuts, bolts and washers larger than M8 (metric thread size) and small cast iron/steel and forged steel components of various geometries. The materials from which they are made are likely to change significantly with little guarantee of composition, as cast components may well be made from remelted scrap and fasteners machined from feedstock of unknown composition. There will also be a requirement to galvanize small fabrications of sheet, tube, bar, section and plate steel.

The maximum mass of parts to be galvanized is likely to be 0.25 tonnes/hour (smallest size generally used). Ultimately, the smallest economical kettle size will be determined by a series of comparative discounted cash flow forecasts using different kettle sizes, and will depend on achieving an acceptable level of profitability. Again, without access to real market conditions, this is impossible to determine, so 0.25 tonnes per hour has been supplied from discussions with galvanizing consultants and plant suppliers.

The as-supplied condition of the components for galvanizing will be variable: the fasteners will be contaminated with light grease and cutting oil, the fabrications often contaminated with paint and weld spatter, the castings with sand.

It is assumed that the average mix of components is comprised of:

- 60 per cent fasteners
- 30 per cent castings
- 10 per cent fabrications

For this type of mix, experience suggests that the zinc consumed will be approximately 8 per cent of the workload mass, i.e. 0.08 tonnes zinc per tonne of work. It is also assumed that there is no market for sale of the zinc-containing dross, skimmings and ash that make up a significant proportion of the 8 per cent.

It is assumed that after the initial increase in production rate to a maximum 0.25 tonnes/hour has been achieved, utilization will be a function of plant maintenance as market demand is greater than the capacity of the plant. The minimum standard of workmanship, or product specification, has been assumed to be BS729.

Process specification

Based upon the assumptions defined above and using the information in Section I, the process specification can be determined. An adequate process flow chart for this mix of components and throughput is described in Figure 29. The process specified is reasonably comprehensive and it may be possible to remove or add process steps to optimize the galvanizing activity to suit specific circumstances.

Plant specification

The rate of throughput will be limited by the slowest process stage, and the exact floor to floor times between process stages will have to be determined through experiment during trials and operation. On this basis the galvanizing plant has been designed with an element of flexibility. Table 6 describes the plant specification in detail and Figures 30 and 31 are diagrammatic representations of typical plant layouts. This is not a basic minimum of equipment but will be flexible enough to accom-

Table 6: Detailed plant specification

Item no.	Description	Approximate dimensions (mm)			Approximate fluid capacity (litres)	Comments
		Length	Width	Depth		
1	Alkaline degreasing tank	1000	1000	1200	1000	requires heating from heat exchanger and boiler units (items 15 and 16) via lagged pipes and steam coils fabricated from mild steel
2	Rinse tank	1000	1000	1200	1000	access to water is required for topping up and changing; there is an option to have two rinse tanks, the first containing hot water: if this is chosen its specification should be as item 1
3	HCl pickle tank	1250	1000	1200	1100	contains 28% HCl
4	HCl pickle tank	1250	1000	1200	1100	contains 28% HCl + equal volume of water
5	HCl stripping tank	1250	1000	1200	1100	contains used and discarded pickle solution to strip existing zinc off items requiring rework
6	Rinse tank	1000	1000	1200	1000	alternative design can include two tanks, the second using the overflow from the first: a more economical method of conserving water
7	Drying deck	1500	1000			perforated cast iron on a suitable plinth, heated by waste gases from kettle passing underneath
8	5-tonne galvanizing kettle	1200	750	1200		oil, gas or electrically heated, operating at 2 years at a time; recommend purchase including control systems from specialist supplier
9	Single basket centrifuge	500 diameter		1000		must achieve rotational speed of approximately 450 rpm in 2 to 3 seconds; zinc is recovered manually and returned to the kettle
10	Quench tank (Bosh)	1300	1000	1200	650	requires a water temperature control between 20 and 50°C; to facilitate this, connection to running water may be required
11	Waste heat exhaust	specified by kettle supplier				refer to relevant environmental, health and safety data
12	Fume extraction unit	specified by kettle supplier				refer to relevant environmental, health and safety data
13	Overhead monorail	8000				complete with either single speed motorized hoist or manual block and tackle
14	Circular monorail					as above but with 2-speed motorized hoist or suitably geared block and tackle to facilitate fast immersion and slow removal of components from the kettle and rapid transfer to the bosh
15	Boiler unit	specified by kettle supplier				supplementary heating system linked to item 16
16	Heat exchanger	specified by kettle supplier				situated on take-off from main flue to heat water for item 1; temperature control is linked to boiler operation, item 15
17	Master control unit	specified by kettle supplier				used for temperature control of the kettle
18	Ancillary equipment					tongs, zinc pump, various maintenance tools, drossing grab, perforated ladles etc.
19	35kW generator	specified by supplier				used to supply electrical power for lights, blower motor and centrifuge with capacity for extras; there is no reliance on mains power

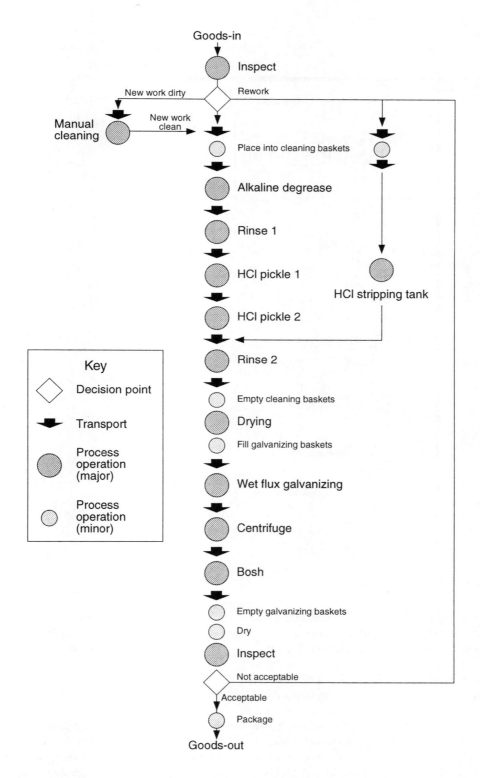

Figure 29: *Process flow chart for the goods-in specification.*

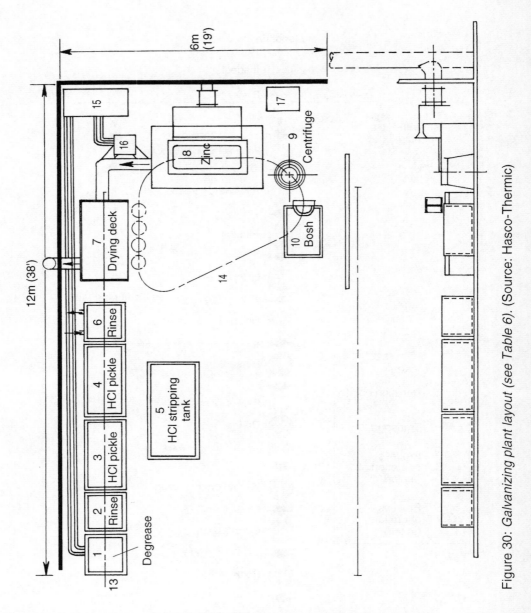

Figure 30: *Galvanizing plant layout (see Table 6).* (Source: Hasco-Thermic)

modate variation in product mix and some increase in throughput if necessary. The plant for this exercise is modelled on Figure 30. In addition to the plant shown on the diagram, containers for zinc will be required along with the usual ancillary equipment described in Section I.

Two sets of baskets will be required, one set for the cleaning stages, the other for the dipping and centrifuging. The use of a single basket would soon render the pickling bath ineffective and result in a high rate of

zinc loss as the zinc picked up from the bath during each dip by the basket would then be stripped during immersion in the acid.

Monorail

An overhead monorail is the simplest method of controlling work flow. Manual operation is possible but hand-dipping is normally reserved for buckets and similar hollow-ware products galvanized in small batches. Another option would be to limit

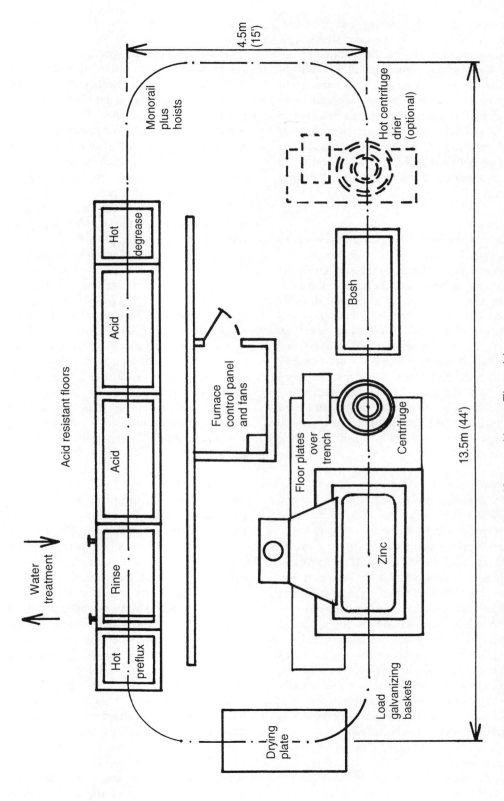

Figure 31: *Proposed layout for nail galvanizing plant.* (Source: Hasco-Thermic)

the monorail to the dipping and centrifuging activities. This is the crucial stage, as delay in the transfer of the workload from the kettle to the centrifuge allows solidification of the excess zinc, and subsequent expensive rework. For cleaning and pickling, smaller manually handled baskets can be fabricated, walked through the processes and emptied on to the drying deck. The choice between these options is best made by evaluating the cost savings and quality issues.

Drying deck
The wet flux method allows components to be dipped while wet, as the flux blanket removes any water from the surface of the components before submersion in the zinc. However, the cost of a drying deck is relatively low, so there is little saving, and an area is required for basket changing. There is also a danger of molten zinc splashes if the flux blanket is not properly maintained and water does come into contact with the zinc. In addition, the drying deck can be heated by waste gases, and therefore makes the dipping process more energy-efficient (if gas- or oil-fired heating is employed).

Heating system
The heating system for the degreasing process and the drying deck uses the waste heat generated from the galvanizing kettle plus supplemental heating from a boiler unit (similar to those used in European domestic heating systems). This is a key reason for choosing either gas or oil kettle heating, as electrical heating does not produce waste heat in significant amounts. Normally waste gases are taken through a by-pass from the exhaust flue within which a heat exchanger is housed. The flue by-pass opening is controlled by a sensor monitoring the water temperature in the heat exchanger unit. It is this water which is supplemented by the boiler unit.

Water tanks
Where flooding is a regular or potential problem, the tanks may be set on blocks above floor level. This also reduces the chances of accidents.

The equipment list specifies static water rinse tanks. Running water is preferable but unless massive water losses can be sustained, a water treatment and recycling plant will be necessary. This treatment plant introduces another technology which may not be appropriate in some developing environments. Information about this type of plant can be obtained from the galvanizing plant suppliers if required.

The use of static water tanks demands extra vigilance on the part of the plant operators as the water pH will have to be monitored regularly. Neutrality of the second rinse tank (after the acid pickle) can be maintained by adding ammonia, but this is not possible with the rinse following the alkaline degrease. This makes estimates of water usage very difficult, and if the costs of water are disproportionately high compared with the total cost in the profitability analysis, these estimates should be reviewed. The same goes for the regularity of acid replacement, as this will depend heavily on the quality and condition of the workload, which is impossible to predict accurately.

Control system
Although most of the plant is technologically quite simple, the control system used to regulate the temperature of the zinc (and possibly the other temperature-sensitive process steps) is often electronic in nature, controlling servo-mechanical devices. These operate baffle valves controlling air flow in oil-fuelled systems and gas flow in gas-fuelled systems, using signals generated by thermocouple sensors immersed in the molten zinc. For electrically powered systems there is no need for mechanical devices. This type of technology is not necessarily appropriate for industrially developing countries. Simpler semi-manual methods can be adopted for maintaining satisfactory plant operation but they undoubtedly require much more vigilant activity by operators and technicians, and are subject to a greater degree of human

judgement (manual temperature monitoring and control). On the other hand, the introduction of inappropriate technology, its subsequent failure and the inability to repair it will also debilitate the manufacturing enterprise.

It is the responsibility of the project engineer to decide on the type of control system most suited to the environment within which the technology is to be placed. It is interesting to note that only 30 years ago galvanizing kettles were being fired by coke with no temperature control whatsoever. Usually, the plant manager would have a spare kettle available and be able to estimate the time of failure through experience (in one reported case the failure rate was once every four months). Nevertheless, every four months a large proportion of the molten zinc was lost and accidents were common.

Typically, electrically powered systems are cheap to install but expensive to run, while both gas and oil tend to be the opposite. Gas and oil systems also tend to be more robust; in the event of a perforation, it is common for electrical heating elements to be destroyed while oil and gas burners are left unscathed.

Project life cycle analysis

The purpose of this task is to identify and plan the initial investment and other inputs that will be necessary to maintain the operation of the plant throughout its estimated lifespan. These material and labour inputs will be essentially the same, regardless of the location of the plant, and need to be specified as a function of time and the nature of the requirement, such as whether it is capital or revenue in nature.

To facilitate this, a spreadsheet has been created (Table 7) which is based upon the process equipment specified in Table 6. The lifespan of the project has been determined as eight years, which is the approximate life expectancy of a kettle. Against each process, at yearly intervals, the requirements representing costs to the business have been estimated in terms of:

- Plant and machinery (including maintenance)
- Consumables
- Personnel.

An additional requirement which is applicable to the whole process and merits its own section in the spreadsheet is:

- Land and buildings.

Every effort has been made to apportion the requirements at a process level, thus avoiding unidentified overheads (indirect costs) as much as possible. By doing this, different combinations of plant can be evaluated more easily.

At the beginning of the spreadsheet, the rates of usage of consumables have been estimated to allow both for valid consumption, such as the transfer of zinc on to the component, and the losses attributable to the process, such as carry-over of HCl from the bath when transferring components, and zinc splashes. The operational specifications have also been stated, such as days worked per year and shift lengths.

Profitability analysis

The identified outflows can now be converted into cash terms and from this a cash flow statement can be prepared using Tables 8 and 9. The profitability will now be dependent on the revenue that can be generated from the operation of the plant. Once this has been calculated, discounting (using suitable estimates of interest rates) will provide the profitability of the plant based on the measures of performance demanded. For the purposes of this analysis, the Net Present Value method (NPV) has been used, whereby the galvanizing operation is deemed to be viable if the NPV is greater that zero.

A note on the NPV method of evaluating projects
The NPV method of project evaluation is a specific technique based upon discounted cash flow methods. The decision rule is that an NPV calculated as being greater than

zero suggests that the investment in the project will be profitable. The principle of discounting relies on the time value of money, something that many developing countries are very well aware of. By way of example, at a commercial bank interest rate of 10 per cent, an investment of £1.00 now would yield £1.33 in three years' time. On this basis, £1.33 in three years' time has a present value of £1.00. Similarly, the present value of £1.00 in one year's time is equal to 1.00/1.1 or £0.9091. These present values of future money can be summarized in tables for £1.00 investment at different rates of interest and time in years: see Table 10.

The NPV method discounts the summation of the cash flows annually on a determined interest rate which is equivalent to the finance costs per annum compound. Once the interest rate is determined, the discount factor is taken from Table 10 for the year in question and applied to the annual net cash flow value. The sign of the summation of the annual total NPVs will be positive if the project is profitable.

The difficulty arises in estimating the interest rate (or the required rate of return) as this will vary from company to company and becomes even more difficult when a number of financing sources become involved.

To overcome this, the NPV method can be applied in reverse, and thus the rate of return that a project will produce can be calculated. This is termed the IRR method (Internal Rate of Return). In other words, what discount rate will reduce the sum of the values of the annual net cash flows to exactly the sum of the investment over the operational lifetime of the project? This is conducted by trial and error, using progressively higher discount rates until the NPV is equal or close to zero. If a project yielded a 16 per cent IRR, then it would be profitable if financing costs were less than this figure. The difference between the two is the measure of profitability. In conclusion, if the NPV = 0 or the IRR is equal to the financing rate, then the project is financially self-sustaining.

Notes on the calculations related to materials and labour requirements

General assumptions
It is assumed that a gradual increase in productivity will occur, shown by the percentage of plant utilization and, in the last year of the project, a slight decline in productivity to reflect the age of the plant. No contingency for disposal value of property has been incorporated.

Labour requirements
In the first year, only 25 per cent of the eventual staff will be required, the other 75 per cent being recruited on initiation of production activities.

Alkaline degrease consumables
These costs are calculated assuming an initial tank fill and complete renewal every four years but a topping-up rate equivalent to one litre per tonne of work processed, rounded up to the nearest hundred litres. The effluent requiring disposal will only be that remaining after solution change, as the other losses are due to carry-over and spillage and are not contained.

Rinse tank 1
It is assumed that the water in the tank will require regular replacement, in this case twice a month plus the initial fill. The regular replacement precludes the need for significant topping-up. It is assumed that the rinse solution will not be treated as effluent and no disposal charge is applied.

HCl pickle tank 1
This can be calculated on the same basis as the alkaline degrease process except that the solution is changed annually.

HCl pickle tank 2
As for HCl pickle tank 1 except that the solution is half the concentration in tank 2.

Rinse tank 2
As for rinse tank 1 except that the water can be neutralized by adding ammonia, therefore extending the life of the solution.

Galvanizing bath

Zinc replacement is calculated at 8 per cent of the workload processed. This includes losses in dross, ash and skimmings as well as the coating. Flux replacement rate is calculated as 3kg per shift, replacement occurring at the end of every shift. The energy required is calculated as being 500MJ per tonne of work processed, which assuming a 60 per cent fuel-to-heat conversion efficiency is equivalent to approximately 5 litres/hour for diesel fuel. The energy required by the blower fan is supplied by the generator and is costed under that heading. Approximately 40 per cent of the zinc consumed is assumed to be entrapped or otherwise combined with dross and other waste products.

Maintenance of the bath (kettle) by outside contractors will be necessary every two years for inspection and remedial treatment.

Centrifuge

No energy costs are shown as they are covered by the generator.

Bosh or quench tank

The fluid (water) replacement is necessary only to replace that lost by evaporation and carry-over, plus the initial fill.

Generator

The power rating of the generator has been calculated as 35kVA (kW). It is assumed that the generator will supply the 2kW power requirement for lighting (25 80W fluorescent lights), 1kW for the blower fan and 3kW for the high torque centrifuge motor. The nature of diesel-fuelled alternator sets demands a factored increase of the power rating to arrive at the required 35kW for a 3-phase unit (including excess capacity for unspecified equipment). At an efficiency rating of about 30 per cent, this type of generator will consume approximately 10 litres of diesel fuel per hour.

Miscellaneous equipment

This includes the items 11–18 in Table 6, plus tools (grabbers, pumps etc) and chemical additives such as frothing agents, inhibitors and alloying element additions tin and aluminium (Sn, Al).

Table 7: Materials and labour requirements planning (Project life cycle analysis)

Operational factors

throughput/hour	0.25 tonnes	days worked/year	240	indirect labour (man-days/day)	1
maximum throughput/year	960.00 tonnes	direct labour (man-days/day)	9	plant life expectancy (years)	8
number of working shifts/day	2	(4 men working shift,1 watchman		total annual hours direct labour	17280
length of shifts (hours)	8	on non-operational 3rd shift)		total annual hours indirect labour	1920

Time (years)	-1	0	1	2	3	4	5	6	7
General assumptions									
plant utilization (%)	0	40	60	75	75	75	75	75	50
work processed (tonnes)	0	384	576	720	720	720	720	720	480
scrap rate (%)	0	25	15	10	10	10	10	10	10
Land and buildings									
purchase	✔								
civil works	✔								
rates and charges		✔	✔	✔	✔	✔	✔	✔	✔
Labour requirements									
direct labour (%)	25	100	100	100	100	100	100	100	100
indirect labour (%)	100	100	100	100	100	100	100	100	100

Process stage

1. Alkaline degrease

	-1	0	1	2	3	4	5	6	7
Plant and equipment									
capital investment	✔								
Consumables									
fluid replacement (litres)		1400	600	800	1800	800	800	800	500
spares and repairs (% of capital investment)			5		5		5		5
Effluent disposal									
effluent produced (litres)		1000			1000				1000

2. Rinse tank 1

	-1	0	1	2	3	4	5	6	7
Plant and equipment									
capital investment	✔								
Consumables									
fluid replacement (litres)		13000	19400	24800	24800	24800	24800	24800	16500
spares and repairs (% of capital investment)			5		5		5		5
Effluent disposal									
effluent produced (litres)	0	13000	19000	24000	24000	24000	24000	24000	17000

3. HCl pickle tank 1

	-1	0	1	2	3	4	5	6	7
Plant and equipment									
capital investment	✔								
Consumables									
fluid replacement (litres)	0	1400	1600	1800	1800	1800	1800	1800	1500
spares and repairs (% of capital investment)			5		5		5		5
Effluent disposal									
effluent produced (litres)	0	1000	1000	1000	1000	1000	1000	1000	2000

4. HCl pickle tank 2

	-1	0	1	2	3	4	5	6	7
Plant and equipment									
capital investment	✔								
Consumables									
fluid replacement (litres)	0	1400	1600	1800	1800	1800	1800	1800	1500
spares and repairs (% of capital investment)			5		5		5		5
Effluent disposal									
effluent produced (litres)	0	1000	1000	1000	1000	1000	1000	1000	2000

5. Rinse tank 2

	-1	0	1	2	3	4	5	6	7
Plant and equipment									
capital investment	✔								
Consumables									
fluid replacement		7000	10000	12800	12800	12800	12800	12800	8500
spares and repairs (% of capital investment)			5		5		5		5
Effluent disposal									
effluent		7000	10000	12800	12800	12800	12800	12800	9500

Continued...

Table 7 (continued): Materials and labour requirements planning (Project life cycle analysis)

Time (years)	-1	0	1	2	3	4	5	6	7
6. Drying deck									
Plant and equipment									
capital investment	✔								
spares and repairs (% of capital investments)			5		5		5		5
7. Galvanizing bath									
Plant and equipment									
capital investment	✔								
Consumables									
zinc replacement (tonnes)	5	31	46	58	58	58	58	58	39
flux replacement (kg)	50	1500	1500	1500	1500	1500	1500	1500	1500
spares and repairs (% of capital investments)			5		5		5		5
Power									
energy required (litres fuel oil)	0	17500	26500	33000	33000	33000	33000	33000	22000
Effluent disposal									
dross (tonnes)		12	17	22	22	22	22	22	14
Maintenance (outside contractors)									
man-days required (excluding installation)			10		10		10		10
8. Centrifuge									
Plant and equipment									
capital investment	✔								
Consumables									
spares and repairs (% of capital investments)			5		5		5		5
9. Bosh									
Plant and equipment									
capital investment	✔								
Consumables									
fluid replacement (litres)	650	400	600	800	800	800	800	800	500
spares and repairs (% of capital investments)			5		5		5		5
10. Generator									
Plant and equipment									
capital investment	✔								
energy required (litres fuel oil)	44000	88000	88000	88000	88000	88000	88000	88000	88000
Consumables									
spares and repairs (% of capital investments)			5		5		5		5
11. Miscellaneous equipment									
Plant and equipment (Items 11 to 18 in Table 6)									
capital investment	✔								
Consumables									
i chemical agents etc	20	20	20	20	20	20	20	20	20
ii									
iii									
iv									
v									
spares and repairs (% of capital investments)			5		5		5		5

Table 8: Checklist of cost data required for the profitability analysis

	Pound sterling (£)
Land and buildings	
purchase	75000
civil works	35000
rates and charges	200/week
Labour requirements	
direct labour rates	av. 15000/person/year
indirect labour rates (e.g. accountant)	av. 150000/person/year
Process stage	
1. Alkaline degrease	
capital investment	500
residual value	
alkali solution cost	0.031/litre
effluent disposal cost	0.0004/litre
2. Rinse tank 1	
capital investment	180
residual value	
water cost	0.001/litre
effluent disposal cost	
3. HCl pickle tank 1	
capital investment	250
residual value	
acid solution cost	0.09/litre
effluent disposal cost	0.0004/litre
4. HCl pickle tank 2	
capital investment	250
residual value	
acid solution cost	0.044/litre
effluent disposal cost	0.0004/litre
5. Rinse tank 2	
capital investment	180
residual value	
water cost	0.001/litre
effluent disposal cost	
6. Drying deck	
capital investment	200
residual value	
7. Galvanizing bath	
capital investment	38000
residual value	5000
zinc cost	850/tonne
flux cost	0.9/kg
oil cost	0.44/litre
dross disposal cost	0.005/kg
maintenance cost	500/day
8. Centrifuge	
capital investment	2300
residual value	500
9. Bosh	
capital investment	180
residual value	
water cost	0.001/litre
10. Generator	
capital investment	8500
residual value	2000
fuel cost	0.44/litre
11. Miscellaneous equipment	
capital investment	16000
residual value	

Table 9: Profitability analysis (all costs in £ Sterling)

Operational factors

throughput/hour	0.25 tonnes	days worked/year	240	indirect labour (man-days/day)	1
maximum throughput/year	960.00 tonnes	direct labour (man-days/day)	9	plant life expectancy (years)	8
number of working shifts/day	2	(4 men/working shift, 1 watchman		total annual hours direct labour	17280
length of shifts (hours)	8	on non-operational 3rd shift)		total annual hours indirect labour	1920

Time (years)	-1	0	1	2	3	4	5	6	7	Row totals
General assumptions										
plant utilization (%)	0	40	60	75	75	75	75	75	50	
work processed (tonnes)	0	384	576	720	720	720	720	720	480	
scrap rate (%)	0	25	15	10	10	10	10	10	10	
Land and buildings										
purchase	75000									75000
civil works	35000									35000
rates and charges		10400	10400	10400	10400	10400	10400	10400	10400	83200
Labour requirements										
direct labour	45000	135000	135000	135000	135000	135000	135000	135000	135000	1125000
indirect labour	15000	15000	15000	15000	15000	15000	15000	15000	15000	135000

Process stage

1. Alkaline degrease

	-1	0	1	2	3	4	5	6	7	Row totals
Plant and equipment										
capital investment	500									500
Consumables										
fluid replacement		43.4	18.6	24.8	55.8	24.8	24.8	24.8	15.5	232.5
spares and repairs			25		25		25		25	100
Effluent disposal										
effluent		0.4			0.4				0.4	1.2

2. Rinse tank 1

	-1	0	1	2	3	4	5	6	7	Row totals
Plant and equipment										
capital investment	180									180
Consumables										
fluid replacement		13	19.4	24.8	24.8	24.8	24.8	24.8	16.5	172.9
spares and repairs			9		9		9		9	36
Effluent disposal										
effluent	0	0	0	0	0	0	0	0	0	0

3. HCl pickle tank 1

	-1	0	1	2	3	4	5	6	7	Row totals
Plant and equipment										
Capital investment	250									250
Consumables										
fluid replacement	0	126	144	162	162	162	162	162	135	1215
spares and repairs			12.5		12.5		12.5		12.5	50
Effluent disposal										
effluent	0	0.4	0.4	0.4	0.4	0.4	0.4	0.4	0.8	3.6

4. HCl pickle tank 2

	-1	0	1	2	3	4	5	6	7	Row totals
Plant and equipment										
capital investment	250									250
Consumables										
fluid replacement	0	61.6	70.4	79.2	79.2	79.2	79.2	79.2	66	594
spares and repairs			12.5		12.5		12.5		12.5	50
Effluent disposal										
effluent	0	0.4	0.4	0.4	0.4	0.4	0.4	0.4	0.8	3.6

5. Rinse tank 2

	-1	0	1	2	3	4	5	6	7	Row totals
Plant and equipment										
capital investment	180									180
Consumables										
fluid replacement		7	10	12.8	12.8	12.8	12.8	12.8	8.5	89.5
spares and repairs			9		9		9		9	36
Effluent disposal										
effluent	0	0	0	0	0	0	0	0	0	0

Continued...

Table 9 (Continued): Profitability analysis

Time (years)	-1	0	1	2	3	4	5	6	7	Row totals
6. Drying deck										
Plant and equipment										
capital investment	200									200
spares and repairs			5		5		5		5	20
7. Galvanizing bath										
Plant and equipment										
capital investment	38000									38000
Consumables										
zinc replacement	4250	26350	39100	49300	49300	49300	49300	49300	33150	349350
flux replacement	45	1350	1350	1350	1350	1350	1350	1350	1350	10845
spares and repairs			1900		1900		1900		1900	7600
Power										
energy cost	0	7700	11660	14520	14520	14520	14520	14520	9680	101640
Effluent disposal										
dross		60	85	110	110	110	110	110	70	765
Maintenance (outside contractors)										
cost			5000		5000		5000		5000	20000
8. Centrifuge										
Plant and equipment										
capital investment	2300									2300
Consumables										
spares and repairs			115		115		115		115	460
9. Bosh										
Plant and equipment										
capital investment	180								180	
Consumables										
fluid replacement	0.65 0.4		0.6	0.8	0.8	0.8	0.8	0.5	6.15	
spares and repairs			9		9		9		9	36
10. Generator										
Plant and equipment										
capital investment	8500									8500
energy	19360	38720	38720	38720	38720	38720	38720	38720	38720	329120
Consumables										
spares and repairs			425		425		425		425	1700
11. Miscellaneous equipment										
Plant and equipment (Items 11 to 18 in Table 6)										
capital investment	16000									16000
Consumables										
i chemical agents etc	20	270	270	270	270	270	270	270	270	2180
ii										0
iii										0
iv										0
v										0
spares and repairs			800		800		800		800	3200
Annual costs (column totals)	260215.7	243357.6	268425.8	273230.2	281583.6	273230.2	281552.2	273230.2	260461	
Estimated annual revenue selling at £ 512 per tonne	0	196608	294912	368640	368640	368640	368640	368640	245760	
Gross cash flow (£)	-260216	-46749.6	26486.2	95409.8	87056.4	95409.8	87087.8	95409.8	-14701	
Cumulative profit (£)	-260216	-306965	-280479	-185069	-98012.9	-2603.05	84484.75	179894.6	165193.6	
Discounted at 10%	-260216	-42500.1	21888.2	71681.38	59459.52	59239.94	49161.06	48964.31	-6858.02	

Net Present Value (NPV) = the sum of the annual discounted net cash flows = 820.689
Please note that by raising the sales price/tonne to £550, the NPV figure is raised to 126399.6. However, this is a very high charge rate.

Table 10: Discount table

Source: Open University

Years	1%	2%	3%	4%	5%	6%	7%	8%	9%	10%	11%	12%	13%	14%	15%	16%
1	0.9901	0.9804	0.9709	0.9615	0.9524	0.9434	0.9346	0.9259	0.9174	0.9091	0.9009	0.8929	0.8850	0.8772	0.8696	0.8621
2	0.9803	0.9612	0.9426	0.9246	0.9070	0.8900	0.8734	0.8573	0.8471	0.8264	0.8116	0.7972	0.7831	0.7695	0.7561	0.7432
3	0.9706	0.9423	0.9151	0.8890	0.8638	0.8396	0.8163	0.7938	0.7722	0.7513	0.7312	0.7118	0.6931	0.6750	0.6575	0.6407
4	0.9610	0.9238	0.8835	0.8548	0.8227	0.7921	0.7629	0.7350	0.7084	0.6830	0.6587	0.6355	0.6133	0.5921	0.5718	0.5523
5	0.9515	0.9057	0.8626	0.8219	0.7835	0.7473	0.7130	0.6806	0.6499	0.6209	0.5935	0.5674	0.5428	0.5194	0.4972	0.4761
6	0.9420	0.8830	0.8375	0.7903	0.7462	0.7050	0.6663	0.6302	0.5963	0.5645	0.5346	0.5066	0.4803	0.4556	0.4323	0.4104
7	0.9327	0.8706	0.8131	0.7599	0.7107	0.6651	0.6227	0.5835	0.5470	0.5132	0.4817	0.4523	0.4251	0.3996	0.3759	0.3538
8	0.9235	0.8535	0.7894	0.7307	0.6768	0.6274	0.5820	0.5403	0.5019	0.4665	0.4339	0.4039	0.3762	0.3506	0.3269	0.3050
9	0.9143	0.8368	0.7664	0.7026	0.6446	0.5919	0.5439	0.5002	0.4604	0.4241	0.3909	0.3606	0.3329	0.3075	0.2843	0.2630
10	0.9053	0.8203	0.7441	0.6756	0.6139	0.5584	0.5083	0.4632	0.4224	0.3855	0.3522	0.3220	0.2946	0.2697	0.2472	0.2267
11	0.8963	0.8043	0.7224	0.6496	0.5847	0.5268	0.4751	0.4289	0.3875	0.3505	0.3173	0.2875	0.2607	0.2366	0.2149	0.1954
12	0.8874	0.7885	0.7014	0.6246	0.5568	0.4970	0.4440	0.3971	0.3555	0.3186	0.2858	0.2567	0.2307	0.2076	0.1869	0.1685
13	0.8787	0.7730	0.6810	0.6006	0.5303	0.4688	0.4150	0.3677	0.3262	0.2897	0.2575	0.2292	0.2042	0.1821	0.1625	0.1452
14	0.8700	0.7579	0.6611	0.5775	0.5051	0.4423	0.3878	0.3405	0.2992	0.2633	0.2320	0.2046	0.1807	0.1597	0.1413	0.1252
15	0.8613	0.7430	0.6419	0.5553	0.4810	0.4173	0.3624	0.3152	0.2745	0.2394	0.2090	0.1827	0.1599	0.1401	0.1229	0.1079

n	17%	18%	19%	20%	21%	22%	23%	24%	25%	26%	27%	28%	29%	30%	31%	32%
1	0.8547	0.8475	0.8403	0.8333	0.8264	0.8197	0.8130	0.8065	0.8000	0.7937	0.7874	0.7813	0.7752	0.7692	0.7634	0.7576
2	0.7305	0.7182	0.7062	0.6944	0.6830	0.6719	0.6610	0.6504	0.6400	0.6299	0.6200	0.6104	0.6009	0.5917	0.5827	0.5739
3	0.6244	0.6086	0.5934	0.5787	0.5646	0.5507	0.5374	0.5245	0.5120	0.4999	0.4882	0.4768	0.4658	0.4552	0.4448	0.4348
4	0.5337	0.5158	0.4987	0.4823	0.4665	0.4514	0.4369	0.4230	0.4096	0.3968	0.3844	0.3725	0.3611	0.3501	0.3396	0.3294
5	0.4561	0.4371	0.4190	0.4019	0.3855	0.3700	0.3552	0.3411	0.3277	0.3149	0.3027	0.2910	0.2799	0.2693	0.2592	0.2495
6	0.3898	0.3704	0.3521	0.3349	0.3186	0.3033	0.2888	0.2751	0.2621	0.2499	0.2383	0.2274	0.2170	0.2072	0.1979	0.1890
7	0.3332	0.3139	0.2959	0.2791	0.2633	0.2486	0.2348	0.2218	0.2097	0.1983	0.1877	0.1776	0.1682	0.1594	0.1510	0.1432
8	0.2848	0.2660	0.2487	0.2326	0.2176	0.2038	0.1909	0.1789	0.1678	0.1574	0.1478	0.1388	0.1304	0.1226	0.1153	0.1085
9	0.2434	0.2255	0.2090	0.1938	0.1799	0.1670	0.1552	0.1443	0.1342	0.1249	0.1164	0.1084	0.1011	0.0943	0.0830	0.0822
10	0.2080	0.1911	0.1756	0.1615	0.1486	0.1369	0.1262	0.1164	0.1074	0.0992	0.0916	0.0847	0.0784	0.0725	0.0672	0.0623
11	0.1778	0.1619	0.1476	0.1346	0.1228	0.1122	0.1026	0.0938	0.0859	0.0787	0.0721	0.0662	0.0607	0.0558	0.0513	0.0472
12	0.1520	0.1372	0.1240	0.1122	0.1015	0.0920	0.0834	0.0757	0.0687	0.0625	0.0568	0.0517	0.0471	0.0429	0.0392	0.0357
13	0.1299	0.1163	0.1042	0.0935	0.0839	0.0754	0.0678	0.0610	0.0550	0.0496	0.0447	0.0404	0.0365	0.0330	0.0299	0.0271
14	0.1110	0.0985	0.0876	0.0779	0.0693	0.0618	0.0551	0.0492	0.0440	0.0393	0.0352	0.0316	0.0283	0.0253	0.0228	0.0205
15	0.0949	0.0835	0.0736	0.0649	0.0573	0.0507	0.0448	0.0397	0.0352	0.0312	0.0277	0.0247	0.0219	0.0195	0.0174	0.0155

Notes on accidents and hazards

The following are examples of serious accidents that have occurred in galvanizing plants around the world:

- Lacerations, cuts and bruises from poor stacking and storage of work.
- Crushing of workers by poorly supervised transport of work using overhead hoists and gantries.
- Fatal falls into caustic, acid and galvanizing baths.
- The loss of limbs from accidental immersion in caustic, acid and galvanizing baths.
- Fatal and debilitating explosions from incorrect mixing of alkali solutions.
- Burns from acid and alkali solutions, and molten zinc.
- Chronic skin disorders from contact with chemicals.

- Metal fume fever.
- Fatal and debilitating explosions from dipping work with sealed sections containing air.
- Fatal and debilitating explosions caused by vaporization of liquid trapped in the workload during dipping in the molten zinc.
- Fatalities and serious accidents from poorly designed ancillary equipment such as skimmers.
- Asphyxiation as a result of poor ventilation and low ceilings.

It is therefore essential that the safety notes are read carefully and all precautions observed. Good planning and management should ensure that operators do not take unnecessary risks and are not placed in dangerous conditions.

Further reading

The following publications are among those available from the Galvanizers' Association, UK (see address on page 63).

Steelwork Corrosion Protection Guide (Exterior)

Steelwork Corrosion Protection Guide (Interior)

Galvanizing in Action: Fasteners

The Engineers and Architects Guide to Hot-dip Galvanizing

Hot-Dip Galvanizing – International journal for users of galvanizing, a periodical printed in English, German, French and Spanish, available on annual subscription.

Galvanizing, Heinz Bablick – The definitive text on galvanizing

Advisory services

United Kingdom

The Galvanizers' Association
GA was set up in 1949 and comprises the leading galvanizing companies in the UK and others throughout the world. In the UK more than 90% of work is processed by members and internationally there are over 50 overseas members in 28 countries.

The GA is a non-profit-making organization formed to promote hot-dip-galvanized steel and provide a service of technical advice and information to producers and users.

This information and advice is generally available free of charge.

Europe

European General Galvanizers' Association
The Galvanizers' Association is affiliated to the Zinc Development Association (ZDA) and based in the same offices in London. The ZDA is also the Secretariat for the European General Galvanizers Association (EGGA), which brings together galvanizing association representatives from Europe. Individual country contacts are listed below:

Austria
Fachverband der Eisen- und
   Metallwarenindustrie Osterreichs
Wiedner Haupstrasse 63
Postfach 335, A-1045 Vienna

Tel: (+432) 22 65 05
Telex: 113872 FVEM A

Belgium
ProGalva
47 rue Montoyer, B-1040 Brussels

Tel: (+323) 513 8634
Telex: 22077 CNOFER B

France
Galvanzinc Association –
   Association Française
   pour la Développement
   de la galvanisation
101 rue Jean-Jaurès
92307 Levallois-Perret

Tel: (+331) 4739 47 40
Telex: 611843
Fax: (+331) 4270 92 67

Germany FR
Verband der Deutschen
   Feuerverzinkungsindustrie eV (VDF)
Sohnstrasse 70
D-4000 Düsseldorf

Tel: (+49 211) 679 00 04
Telex: 0858685 GUSS D
Fax: (+49 211) 687 13 33

Italy
Associazione Italiana Zincatura
Piazza Sant 'Agostino 18
20123 Milan

Tel: (+39 2) 43 52 15/43 44 12

The Netherlands
Stichting Doelmatig Verzinken
Hoofdstraat 213
2171 BC Sassenheim

Tel: (+31 70) 24 50 85

Portugal

> Associacao Portugese
> de Galvanizacao
> Rue do Campo Alegre, 672-2 Esq
> Porto

Spain

> Associación Técnica Española
> de Galvanización
> CENIM
> Ciudad Universitaria
> 28040 Madrid
>
> Tel: (+34 1) 253 89 00

Sweden

> Nordisk Forzinkningsförening
> (Nordic Galvanizers)
> Kungsgatan 37, 4tr
> S-111 56 Stockholm
>
> Tel: (+468) 20 80 38

Switzerland

> Vereinigung Schweizerischer
> Verzinkereien
> CH-3011 Bern
> Bundesplatz 4 (Postfach 1761)
>
> Tel: (+41 31) 22 61 51
> Telex: 33569

United Kingdom and Eire

> Galvanizers' Association
> Wren's Court
> 56 Victoria Road
> Sutton Coldfield
> West Midlands B72 1SY
>
> Tel: (+44 121) 355 8838
> Fax: (+44 121) 355 8727

Other zinc and galvanizing associations

Asia

> Zinc and Lead Asian Service
> 124 Exhibition Street
> Melbourne
> Victoria, Australia 3000

Australasia

> Australian Zinc Development
> Association
> 124 Exhibition Street
> Melbourne
> Victoria, Australia 3000

India

> Indian Lead Zinc Information Centre
> B-6/7 Shopping Centre
> Safdarjung Enclave
> New Delhi

Japan

> Japan Lead Zinc
> Development Association
> New Hibiya Building
> 3-6 Uchisaiwaicho
> 1-Chrome, Chiyoda-Ku
> Tokyo 100

South Africa

> South African Hot Dip
> Galvanizers Association
> UWTEC, Box 77
> WITS 2050

USA

> American Hot Dip
> Galvanizers Association
> 1101 Connecticut Avenue, NW
> Suite 700
> Washington DC
> 20036-4303

Relevant standards

Hot-dip galvanizing of iron and steel articles to BS729 is the main standard referred to in this guide (the product specification).

Other national and international standards on hot dip and other zinc coatings are available as listed below.

British Standards

Galvanizing Standards
BS729
  Hot dip galvanized coatings on iron and steel articles
BS443
  Zinc coatings on wire
BS2989
  Hot dip zinc coatings on steel sheet
BS3083
  Hot dip coated corrugated sheet for general purposes

Other zinc coating Standards
BS1706
  Electroplated coating of cadmium and zinc on iron and steel
BS2569: Part 1
  Sprayed aluminium and zinc coatings against corrosion
BS3382: Part 2
  Electroplated zinc on threaded components
BS4921
  Sherardized coatings on iron and steel articles
BS417
  Galvanized mild steel cisterns, covers, tanks and cylinders

Other useful British Standards
CP1021
  Cathodic protection
CP3012
  Cleaning and preparation of metal surfaces
PD6484
  Corrosion at bi-metallic contacts
BS5493
  Code of practice for protection of iron and steel against corrosion
BS4232
  Surface preparation by blast cleaning
BS5411
  Methods of test for metallic and related coatings
BS5750
  Quality systems
DD24
  Protection against corrosion on light steel used in building
BS2451
  Chilled iron shot and grit for grit blasting
BS2015
  Glossary of paint terms
BS3900
  Method of test for paints
BS4395
  High strength friction grip bolts
BS4479
  Design of metal articles to be coated

ASTM Standards
A123
  Hot galvanized coatings on fabricated products

64

A90
    Weight of zinc coating on iron and steel
    articles
A153
    Hot dip galvanized centrifugal
    components
A325
    High strength carbon steel bolts
A490
    High strength alloy steel bolts
A525
    Hot dip galvanized steel
A633
    Electroplated zinc articles

German Standards
DIN267
    Hot dip galvanized fasteners
DIN50975
    Protection by hot dip galvanizing:
    guiding principles
DIN50976
    Requirements and testing hot dip
    galvanized coatings on finished products
DIN50978
    Testing of adhesion of hot dip galva-
    nized coatings
DIN50933
    Measurement of coating thickness using
    dial indicator
DIN50981
    Measurement of coating thickness:
    magnetic method
DIN51213
    Testing of zinc coatings on wire
DIN59231
    Galvanized corrugated sheet
DIN50961
    Electroplating zinc
DIN8565
    Zinc spraying

Swedish Standards
SM53192
    Hot dip galvanized threaded components
SIS055900
    Blast cleaning steel
SMS52950
    Principles and requirements for hot dip
    galvanizing
SNS52952
    Measurement of coating thickness by
    microscopic method
SMS52971
    Measurement of coating thickness by
    magnetic method

International Standards
ISO1459
    Protection by hot dip galvanizing:
    guiding principles
ISO1460
    Determination of hot dip galvanizing
    coating mass: gravimetric method
ISO1461
    Requirements of hot dip galvanized
    coatings on fabricated components
ISO1463
    Measurement of coating thickness:
    microscopic method
ISO2063
    Metal spraying by zinc and aluminium
ISO2064
    Definition and convention concerning
    coating thickness method
ISO2081
    Electroplated zinc coatings
ISO2178
    Measurement of coating thickness:
    magnetic method
ISO3575
    Continuous hot dip galvanized sheet

Case study

Establishing a galvanizing facility from local materials

Dr K Sraku-Lartey, IMME, University of Science and Technology, Kumasi

Ghana has a large informal industrial sector activity and Suame Magazine, an area in Kumasi, Ghana, finds the densest and most active concentration of this sector. The majority of workshops in this sector are engaged in metalwork production, for example cooking pots, food processing equipment, farming implements, spare parts and other metal products to serve a large rural populace. The sector also supplies essential services for national development through the skills of the many workers engaged in the sector.

Skilful though these workers are (through years of apprenticeship), there is a general lack of technical knowledge. There is therefore a lack of appreciation of basic metallurgical principles. In spite of this, metalworking is one of the areas that has witnessed the most impressive advances in recent years. The lack of adequate formal production plants in Ghana and the neighbouring countries in west Africa, and the shortage of imports to meet demand for items such as spare parts, equipment for small-scale food processing and agricultural tools have contributed a lot to the successes in the informal sector. Metalwork production will thus continue to play a vital role in the technological development of Ghana and its neighbours.

Owing to the limited scientific training of these workers, the finishing of metal products leaves a lot to be desired. Metal parts are generally made of mild steel and are not treated against environmental failures in any way. However, a series of visits to workshops in this sector and discussions with artisans by staff of the Metallurgy

Department of the University of Science and Technology, Kumasi, generated interest in metal finishing.

Specifically, ideas regarding finishing processes that would protect metals against corrosion and also enhance the aesthetic value were welcomed by fabricators, who realized that these values would enable their products to compete favourably with imported products.

Judging from the range of products and their applications, it was felt that galvanizing would be the most appropriate process to adopt, a process which was not being practised in Ghana at that time. The Metallurgy Department, therefore, in collaboration with a spare parts fabricator operating at Suame Magazine, decided to develop a low-cost and easier-to-operate galvanizing unit suitable for small parts.

Developing parameters for a galvanizing process

In the process of establishing the hot-dip galvanizing unit (employing relevant information from the literature), the following factors were considered:

- the coating thickness in relation to the time of coating at a constant temperature;
- the coating thickness in relation to varying temperatures of molten zinc bath at a constant time;
- the use of fluxes and how they affect the process;
- precleaning to remove grease, rust and dirt.

67

The following were employed in the process of developing the unit:

- molten zinc prepared from almost pure zinc;
- alkaline solution of NaOH for degreasing;
- fluxing agents made up of NH_4Cl and $ZnCl_2$ solution;
- solution of HCl for descaling.

In the first series of tests, a constant temperature of 470°C was maintained for the molten zinc, and dipping time varied from 0.5 to 7 minutes. The coating thickness was found to vary directly with time. Coatings produced in less than 2 minutes were generally found to be inadequate, dull and less protective than those obtained over more than 2 minutes which were bright and quite protective.

In the second series of tests, dipping time was fixed at 2 minutes, and the temperature varied from 420°C to 500°C. Temperatures from 420°C to about 450°C produced thin coatings which were not very protective. From 460°C onwards, coating was very bright and protective. Temperatures higher than about 470°C produced burnt coatings.

The protective nature of the coating was determined by immersing the galvanized item in water for about 14 days, during which the pH and temperature were monitored.

The galvanizing plant

The next stage in the development was to translate the laboratory results to produce a small commercial galvanizing plant. The site chosen for this was at Kwadaso, a suburb of Kumasi, where a building was made available. The plant was designed to take small items such as bolts and nuts, links, pins and clamps, the maximum size being about 25 by 15 mm.

The precleaning unit and fluxing unit were set up in one room. The steel parts were handled in a metal basket. The melting unit was set up in an adjacent room, and was made up of a simple hearth built from ordinary burnt bricks. The melting pot or kettle was a wheel rim obtained from a 20-tonne truck and adapted for the purpose. It was suspended on the hearth so that both the bottom and side of the pot could be heated at the same time. A door was made in the front of the furnace. Air was brought into the furnace from a mist blower through a port in the side of the furnace. An exhaust was provided at the rear through a 4-inch pipe about 3m high.

The hearth was fired with charcoal and carbonized palm kernel shells, and the rate of burning was controlled by adjusting the air flow. The mist blower operated on oil–petrol mixture, and was intended for areas that could not use electric blowers. Melting usually took about 2 hours of firing, and the melt could be maintained and used for several hours in the day. The method outlined for laboratory work and the parameters determined were successfully employed in the main work. The main difficulties encountered were with protection against the heat and splashes from the zinc kettle. These were solved to some extent by erecting wooden barriers around the hearth and the pot. Another problem was the cracking of the brickwork after a prolonged period of firing.

The unit was, however, successful, and a number of parts produced for the Electricity Corporation of Ghana were treated. Over several days of use it was realized that the unit needed a number of improvements to make operations smooth, increase production, and enable work to be done on larger items, but inevitably such improvements require extra funding, which was unavailable at this stage of the project.

SOME OTHER USEFUL BOOKS FROM INTERMEDIATE TECHNOLOGY PUBLICATIONS

Making Health-care Equipment: Ideas for local design and production
Compiled by Adam Platt and Nicola Carter
Health care practitioners, planners and artisans will find ideas and designs for equipment that can be made locally in relatively small workshops. Alternative materials and fabrication methods are described to meet differing local circumstances.
96pp, 1990, ISBN 1 85339 067 4.

Edge of the Anvil: A resource book for the blacksmith
Jack Andrews
A fascinating introduction to blacksmithing, illustrated with line drawings and photographs, that takes the reader through all the main processes of blacksmithing, from tools and equipment, lighting a fire, welding, splitting, and decorative iron work.
210pp, 1991, ISBN 1 85339 097 6, hardback. ISBN 1 85339 110 7, paperback.

Equipment for Rural Workshops
John Boyd
A guide for anyone who wishes to equip a workshop, from the basic tools required for a one or two person carpentry workshop without power, to the more sophisticated power equipment for both wood and metal working.
94pp, 1986, ISBN 0 903031 45 0.

Making Wheels: A technical manual on wheel manufacture
R.A. Dennis
A low-cost technology which will enable workshops to set up their own facilities and manufacture a range of wheels from standard steel sections. For those familiar with metalworking techniques. Presented with technical drawings and sketches.
160pp, 1992, ISBN 1 85339 141 7.

Please write for a full catalogue to Intermediate Technology Publications, 103-105 Southampton Row, London WC1B 4HH, UK.